Cambridge Elements

Elements in Translation and Interpreting
edited by
Kirsten Malmkjær
University of Leicester

LITERARY EXOPHONIC TRANSLATION

Lúcia Collischonn
University of Greenwich

Shaftesbury Road, Cambridge CB2 8EA, United Kingdom

One Liberty Plaza, 20th Floor, New York, NY 10006, USA

477 Williamstown Road, Port Melbourne, VIC 3207, Australia

314–321, 3rd Floor, Plot 3, Splendor Forum, Jasola District Centre, New Delhi – 110025, India

103 Penang Road, #05-06/07, Visioncrest Commercial, Singapore 238467

Cambridge University Press is part of Cambridge University Press & Assessment, a department of the University of Cambridge.

We share the University's mission to contribute to society through the pursuit of education, learning and research at the highest international levels of excellence.

www.cambridge.org
Information on this title: www.cambridge.org/9781009535410

DOI: 10.1017/9781009535427

© Lúcia Collischonn 2025

This publication is in copyright. Subject to statutory exception and to the provisions of relevant collective licensing agreements, no reproduction of any part may take place without the written permission of Cambridge University Press & Assessment.

When citing this work, please include a reference to the DOI 10.1017/9781009535427

First published 2025

A catalogue record for this publication is available from the British Library

ISBN 978-1-009-53541-0 Hardback
ISBN 978-1-009-53543-4 Paperback
ISSN 2633-6480 (online)
ISSN 2633-6472 (print)

Cambridge University Press & Assessment has no responsibility for the persistence or accuracy of URLs for external or third-party internet websites referred to in this publication and does not guarantee that any content on such websites is, or will remain, accurate or appropriate.

For EU product safety concerns, contact us at Calle de José Abascal, 56, 1°, 28003 Madrid, Spain, or email eugpsr@cambridge.org

Literary Exophonic Translation

Elements in Translation and Interpreting

DOI: 10.1017/9781009535427
First published online: May 2025

Lúcia Collischonn
University of Greenwich
Author for correspondence: Lúcia Collischonn, luciacollischonn@gmail.com

Abstract: This Element explores literary translation into a non-native language (L2 translation), investigating how it has been regarded by Translation Studies, particularly in the anglophone context. L1 directionality (into the translator's L1) remains the norm in the literary translation world, reflecting a systemic bias against the multilingual subject and towards the monolingual. In a post-monolingual paradigm, the notion of a mother tongue has become increasingly problematic. What are the implications of this for directionality in translation? Studies on L2 translation still focus on and privilege the native speaker. Applying the notion of exophony (i.e. writing in a foreign language) to translation (in what is termed exophonic translation), this Element draws on insights from sociolinguistics, Applied Linguistics, translation history, and translator studies to lay the groundwork in advocating for an exophonic, multilingual turn in Translation Studies. To what extent can this change the way L2 translation is approached and studied?

Keywords: translation studies, exophony, L2 translation, sociology of translation, post-nativespeakerism

© Lúcia Collischonn 2025

ISBNs: 9781009535410 (HB), 9781009535434 (PB), 9781009535427 (OC)
ISSNs: 2633-6480 (online), 2633-6472 (print)

Contents

Introduction 1

1 Norms and Gatekeeping in Translation 3

2 Monolingual, Multilingual, and Exophonic 19

3 Translators under the Microscope 42

4 Coda 56

References 58

Introduction

Conducted at the onset of Covid-19, the study faced technological and ethical hurdles, including outdated research protocols and manual transcription of over 18 hours of interviews. Since then, some interviewees have gained significant career traction, winning prestigious literary awards and publishing their own novels. With that in mind, the exophonic translator, who is proud of their exophonic status, has, in the interim, become more of a known figure in literary translation circles. Those who previously hid their non-compliance, or performed a monolingual drag of sorts, have now felt more comfortable owning up to their non-compliant status.

While analysing these interviews, it became more obvious how the theory of translation and translation history and their many rules about what a translation should be, who a translator is, and so on were not matching up with the reality. In the interviews themselves, one could see how the many issues around defining a mother tongue, and L1 or L2 (or even L3, Lx), linguistic identity, belonging, gatekeeping, directionality, fluency, proficiency, all of these became even more complex than any number of literature reviews could even dream of touching upon.

For those reading this Element, we need to agree on some basic assumptions, due to wordcount constraints. These are as follows:

- Translation Studies as an epistemic child of Comparative Literature has understandably based itself on national languages and literatures, but it must evolve, together with Comparative Literature, and dialogue with other areas that are miles past native-speakerism and monolingual bias (such as Applied Linguistics, for example) that is still present and persistent in Translation Studies.
- There is always going to be a limitation in scope, and countless other studies, terms, and contexts that could be included here. One must assume that, no matter the niche topic, there is definitely someone in one of the corners of the globe studying that, and proving your point, but access to these is limited – limited by language barriers, power structures – most of these inherent to scientific dissemination.

You may be a bit confused by the order of contents here. I will attempt to briefly explain these. Exophony, a term that at first held more weight, ended up becoming a sprinkle of terminological glitter on top of much less shiny discussions around language, gatekeeping, and norms in Translation Studies. The explanation of what exophony is and why I am proposing we call L2 literary translation Exophonic translation comes closer to the end of Section 2 because it follows discussions around multilingualism, native-speakerism, and precedes the next section's concluding argument that a look at the person (the translator) is more worth our time than a look at the text they produce, especially so for literary translation. Why the focus on literary? Firstly, because directionality in non-literary or non-artistic contexts is much less of a problem than in areas with more cultural monolingual gatekeeping such as literature. With over a decade of experience as a technical freelance translator for various areas and text types, I have done translation into countless directionalities (including L2-L3), and, although native-speakerism is still used sometimes as a proof of ability in professional contexts, not being a native speaker of the target language has never prevented me from doing contracted translation work into said language. Secondly, but nevertheless heavily interconnected, there has always been a chasm between the self-fashioning of literary translators and their non-literary counterparts; in Section 3, we will see this in a bit more detail, but often literary translators consider themselves, unconsciously or not, superior in craft to the 'working class' translator. With this, often literary translation has a privilege in being seen more as an artistic practice that does not need the technical, linguistic, and years of technical training, but rather a natural word-smith inclination, and a knowledge of at least one foreign language (and often a Western European one, to add prestige), as well as a native-level understanding of the target language, a target language that, in the case of English, has very complex power structures in place. Thirdly, many have discussed the limits of the split between literary and non-literary translation (Newmark, 2001; Rogers, 2015, 2018), and the division is still not entirely agreed upon.

Why exophony? Exophony (i.e. writing in a second language) is not concerned so much with the exophonic text, but more with a combination of the text and the background of the person who wrote it. Similarly, I suggest that exophonic translation does not need to concern itself with comparing two translations – one produced by an L1 speaker of the target language, the other by an exophonic translator – and trying to compare or find fault in one or the other. Instead, it focuses on these translators and their linguistic background as bringing something new and worthwhile to translation, and advocates against the inherent monolingual bias that keeps exophonic translators at the margin. Thus, literary exophonic translation presupposes a preference for sociological Translation Studies as opposed to overtly textual and rule-based studies. It assumes that a translator has a choice in the language they work with; no matter how they came to learn these languages, they still should be allowed to choose the language they express themselves in from their linguistic repertoire. This is, essentially, what we want literary exophonic translators to be able to do. They should be understood and analysed by their approach to the texts, their creative stances, their choices rather than their supposed shortcomings. Perhaps the ideal study would involve a more text-based approach alongside a sociological approach to the translator behind it. However, to shed a light on these practices is only the beginning of a long road towards trying to understand what exactly is literary exophonic translation. Firstly, one must admit it exists and that it adds something to theory and practice of translation, making this kind of translation visible and accepted. Then, and only then, will we start to have enough corpus to offer a more structured and consistent theoretical backing and knowledge around the practice, pointing to future pedagogical tools, robust epistemologies to strengthen a new possibility for how directionality is seen in literary translation. But this, here, is just the start. This Element will not give you an ultimate answer, it is an attempt to start answering the question, and posing a few questions of its own. By presenting a few tenets, different opinions, experiences, and ways of looking into the 'problem' of literary exophonic translation, we may start seeing it less as a problem and more as an epistemological challenge, a challenge that could be taken on by many practitioners hailing from various language backgrounds. With that, we aim at a truly diverse picture to start doing justice to an ever-evolving, complex language context – that of literary translation.

1 Norms and Gatekeeping in Translation

L2 Translation and Directionality in Translation Studies

The practice of translation into a non-mother tongue, or L2 translation, has not received enough attention in Translation Studies as a whole.[1] Translation Studies in general, as a discipline, is largely Western and anglophone, thus many of the authors within it have been fortunate enough to be able to ignore this issue, since this is not a challenge they have had to face. Coming from a Global South country, or less hegemonic language (Brazilian Portuguese), it is easier for me to see the relevance of L2 translation, for a number of reasons. L2 translation is taught in the context of less hegemonic countries and languages almost as much as L1 translation, and both practices find their place in translators' professional lives. Of course, this is much more common in technical and scientific translation, as the demand in these fields is much more dynamic than in literary translation. According to Beeby (1998): 'Directionality only began to be studied at the end of the twentieth century when some scholars in countries

---

[1] There is no terminological consistency when it comes to this practice, and perhaps this is due to it being under-researched and underappreciated in traditional Translation Studies. A discussion around the terminology will find its place in this Element. For practicality, however, I will use the term L2 translation throughout this Element, and you, the reader, can decide if you agree with me that it should be called anything else.

where A→B translation is common practice questioned the assumption (particularly widespread in English-speaking countries) that B→A translation was the only viable professional option' (Beeby, 1998:84).

Even so, the study of L2 translation specifically is not comparable in quality and quantity to the studies and theories centring on L1 translation, both technical and literary. However, from the 1990s onwards, there has been a stronger focus on L2 translation and its differences to the practice of L1 translation into English specifically, and within several frameworks and different fields in Translation Studies. In approaching the practice of translation into a foreign language, there seems to be a lack of terminological consistency. 'L2 translation' (Pavlović, 2007), 'inverse translation', 'service translation' (cf Newmark, 1988:3), and 'translation into a non-mother tongue' (Pokorn, 2005) are some of the many terms used to define this practice.[2] All of them focus on a hierarchy of languages and on direction in translation. In some languages, the terms used to define L2 translation are derogatory (see Petrova). In Brazilian Portuguese as well as in some Francophone contexts, an L2 translation is a 'version' of something, not even deemed translation proper. According to Stewart, in one of the earliest articles to review the L1 translation norm:

> The disparaging connotations of terms adopted in the literature to describe L2 translation would appear to confirm the general impression that this activity constitutes some sort of deviation from the norm. The relevant nomenclature includes: 'indirect translation', 'inverse translation', 'marked translation', 'service translation', and, possibly the unkindest cut of all, 'pedagogical translation' (i.e., no more than an academic exercise, of no value beyond the walls of the classroom). (Stewart, 2001:207)

These recent studies have contributed to the field immensely, by clarifying different but converging issues around the practice and helping to deconstruct preconceived and prejudiced ideas around translation into a non-mother tongue. They have fed on each other, and this mutual dependence is unsurprising given that not enough has been said on the topic. This situation, in turn, means that only a small group of researchers has delved into this under-researched and undervalued area. Such a situation both helps and at the same time makes the translator and/or researcher interested in this topic shy away from probing into it: there is so much to be said, but there is almost no existing theory about it. To make this claim, however, it is necessary to present these studies and how they have contributed to not putting L2 translation in a corner. That is what I aim to do in the following section.

---

[2] The term 'inverse translation' is widely used in texts about directionality, there is no agreement on who coined the term.

(In)visibility of L2 Translation Studies

Not only the practice of literary L2 translation but also the study of it is obscure both in the market and in academia. For that reason, and because of the lack of a coherent terminology for the practice, finding these translations and studies proves a challenge. Now, I would like to point out that there are obvious limitations of scope and access to see how directionality is viewed in other contexts, including when those studies are written in a less widely diffused language, or when these studies are not easily found due to access constraints, different use of keywords, and so on. Another limitation includes the study of L2 translation in other areas, such as in Early Modern and Medieval Studies, history, and so on when the many possible areas that could deal with examples of L2 translation do not properly dialogue and thus drive a wedge into the works of trying to better understand this practice under an interdisciplinary light.

In the real world, translation contracts or codes of good practice and translation ethics often spell out a preference for L1 translation, especially, but not exclusively in relation to, literary translation. One example here would be the UN Nairobi declaration. At the beginning of the declaration, one can find the following definition of translation: 'the term "translation" denotes the transposition of a literary or scientific work, including technical work, from one language into another language' (1976:39). Here we cannot find a directionality. Further on, however, we encounter the following statement: 'a translator should, as far as possible, translate into his own mother tongue or into a language of which he or she has a mastery equal to that of his or her mother tongue' (1976:42). It seems then that even in legal documents pertaining to the act of translation and translation as a profession there is the need to explain that what one means by translation is specifically the translation from a foreign language into the translator's mother tongue. The mother tongue bias shows itself here as it will repeatedly in translation norms.

The L1 translation preference is reflected in many uncontested norms and in implicit views on directionality in the history of Translation Studies. These implicit views and norms must be unpicked, and this implicit discourse that naturalizes the norm of L1 translation ends up forming our ideas about what is natural and what is expected in translation. Within Gideon Toury's proposal of norms in translation, we could consider the L1 translation norm as extratextual; in that it is not contained within the actual translated text or the source text, it is a prescriptive rather than descriptive norm.[3] In this respect, it might be useful to view the L1 translation norm as a 'translation meme', as defined by Chesterman in *The Memes of Translation* (1997). Taking the definition of a meme as the

---

[3] I will go into more detail on Toury's conceptualization of translation norms in Section 3.

cultural equivalent of a gene and, therefore, as a unit of cultural transmission, of mere replication or imitation (Dawkins 1976), memes, in this context, can be viewed as ideas that spread like genes. According to Chesterman, 'ideas that turn out to be good ideas survive; i.e., those that are conducive to the survival of their carriers' (Chesterman, 1997:6). If we take the norm of L1 translation as a translation meme, this idea would have to be a good idea for someone, that is, conducive to the survival of a specific practice or a standard. It is not that difficult to make the connection between the L1 translation meme, in the context of L2 (literary) translation into English' and the survival of the hegemony of the English language and those who are considered its native speakers.[4] Resistance and open adoption of the L1 translation meme may come from an inability to conceive of a different situation, or even a defensive move. Those who benefit from this meme are not necessarily consciously doing so with an aim to uphold this practice. Therefore, studies that either defend or propose to make visible the practice of L2 translation, which is a reality that has been invisible for too long, are trying to break the L1 translation meme.[5] With it, perhaps the idea of L2 translation is conducive to the survival of minor linguistic communities and turns out to be a good idea after all.

An Overview of L2 Translation Studies

It is not difficult to understand why, among scholars of L2 translation, and Translation Studies scholars in general, there are so many academics living a life between languages and cultures. Many of these scholars are non-native speakers of English who, however, work in English-speaking countries and universities or head English-language undergraduate and postgraduate programmes in their native countries (such as Pokorn, Marmaridou, and Zahedi);[6] others, even though native speakers, talk from the point of view of the periphery, the periphery of the empire (such as the Australian scholar Campbell), or even other non-hegemonic languages and cultures (Grosman, McAlester, Kelly, Pavlović). All these scholars have experienced translation into a non-mother tongue. They try to understand why L2 translation, especially of literary texts, has been considered a second-class citizen in the world of

---

[4] This hegemony of the English language, as I put it, is within the context of anglophone Translation Studies and the publishing market in the UK and US, mainly since institutions in these countries are still responsible for judging global speakers of English on their proficiency in standardized English language tests, for example.

[5] They are also trying to break the monolingual *habitus*/bias, which will be discussed more thoroughly in the next section.

[6] Ironically, exophony, that is, writing in a foreign language (Wright, 2008), is heavily present in Translation Studies. English, being the dominant academic language, especially in this field, is the medium through which many non-native academics write their theories of translation.

translation. Native or non-native speakers of English alike, they all write in English, and have studied translation into English from the most varied languages. This small club of L2 translation researchers and the many linguistic and theoretical variations and approaches within the group show that this is a rich area of Translation Studies.

It is important to name the studies that deal with translation into a non-mother tongue and place them in context. The texts in this cluster have different goals, and this is maybe one of the reasons why there is not as of now a unified theory of L2 translation. Some, like Campbell (1998), talk about L2 translation with the aim of looking at the development of translation competence but also to render visible the practice of L2 translation on the outskirts of the empire (in his case, Australia).[7] Others, like McAlester (1992, 2005), use it to look for improved translation assessment criteria for student translators. Marmaridou (1996), one of the first to talk openly about translation out of the mother tongue, presents a study which focuses on understanding and proper translating of conceptual metaphors by native and non-native translators, comparing these two groups. Zahedi (2013) offers a literature review of the different studies on L2 translation, relying heavily on Allison Beeby's definition of directionality (1998) and Beeby's overview of the status of the practice in Translation Studies.

One of the most groundbreaking studies, and one which has received a great deal of attention, is Pokorn's (2005) study of L2 literary translation in the specific case of Slovenia. Like Zahedi, although lengthier and with a practice approach as well, Pokorn delves deep into the problematic of the mother tongue. Her study is divided into different parts. The first part can be seen as a manifesto and offers many good arguments for the adoption of a more flexible, open view of literary L2 translation. The second part, less theoretical and more methodological/practice-based, is specific to existing cases of translation of Slovene literature into English. In Pokorn's own study, which follows her review, native speakers of English were shown these translations. They looked for inaccuracies, unnaturalness, and lack of fluency, and tried to guess which texts were translated by native speakers and which were not. The study proves that L2 translators performed equally well; most readers could not spot the non-native translations. The problems with this study are mainly that these are existing translations, and therefore it is not possible to analyse

---

[7] Australia belongs, in linguist Braj Kachru's definition (1992), to the inner circle of World Englishes. In the three circles of English model, the diffusion of the English language is focused on three concentric circles, from the inner to the outer circles ending on the expanding circle. Belonging to the inner circle are Englishes that were diffused through a first diaspora: Australia, New Zealand, and North America, but also including the crib of the language, the UK. The different colonial processes and timelines of the US and Australia/New Zealand and these countries' current role in geopolitics might explain why at time Australian English, even though belonging to the inner circle, still sees itself in the outskirts of the empire.

directionality from a procedural point of view, nor can one ask the translators for their attitudes and opinions towards the practice of translating into a non-mother tongue. Pokorn also focuses a great deal on a translator's status as native or non-native 'speaker' and on the acceptability of the translated text to native readers of the target language, that is, English. It would be interesting to see texts translated from English into Slovene to see if the perceived naturalness would be the same when received by Slovene native speakers. However, Pokorn makes convincing points that are advantageous when proposing that L2 translation should not be second class.

There have been two conferences and consequently two sets of conference proceedings dedicated entirely to the topic of translation into non-mother tongues: in May 1997 in Ljubljana and the 2002 Forum on Directionality in Translating and Interpreting in Granada. The two conferences generated two books: *Translation into Non-Mother Tongues in Professional Practice and Training* (2000), and *La direccionalidad en traducción e interpretación. Perspectivas teóricas, profesionales y didácticas [Directionality in translation and interpreting. Theoretical, professional, and didactic perspectives]* (2003). The fact that L2 translation has only explicitly been the topic of a few studies in the last two decades goes to show that it is a theme of growing interest, but also that scholars in minority, peripheral, or less-widely diffused language communities have been able to slowly start breaking the mould of Translation Studies in a context which opens more possibilities for the study of cultures, multilingualism, and displacement.

Kelly et al. (2003), the outcome of the 2002 forum in Granada, provides a good number of studies around directionality, specifically translation into L2 or L3, concluding that there is a call for deeper and more empirical knowledge concerning directionality in translation. In the second part, the authors point to a need for more empirical studies backing these findings, as well as a closer connection between directionality and the concept of translation competence. The authors question the obvious distinction between general and specialized translation, arguing in counterpoint for a more general approach to teaching translation sub-competencies that can articulate between one another and so avoid forming overly specialized translators but rather subjects with a more general competence in translation (Beeby; Rodriguez & Schnell; Narvaez, etc.). The authors also call into question the fact that, traditionally, directionality is only thought of when dealing with inverse translation, whereas it is an important component of every act of translation. Part five of Kelly et al. (2003) focuses specifically on translation teaching and the multilingual classroom. In thinking directionality in the traditional, strict way, a multilingual translation class is viewed as presenting many problems. The studies in this part try to test this view. Tsokaktsidu concludes that the presence of exchange/international students in translation classes is positive overall. In Lucas's study focusing on legal translation, he agrees with Tsokaktsidu in concluding that in a multicultural classroom, with multiple counter-directionalities in the group, the diversity of linguistic profiles is positive. Galiano, with a more methodological approach, asserts, however, that the presence of a variety of different L1s in a translation class makes it necessary to adapt the methodology of directionality to the reality of the classroom.

In the collection *Translation into a Non-Mother Tongue* (2000), the proceedings of the 1997 conference in Ljubljana entirely dedicated to L2 translation, we find a varied number of studies on the practice. More theoretical than the works found in Kelly et al. (2003), this Element focuses more on the status of the practice in theoretical Translation Studies and in the contexts of multiculturality and plurilingualism in Eastern Europe, among others. The studies range from the issue of translation competence, sub-competencies and the teaching of genre literacy in translation (Prunč; Kiraly; Bretthauer, Geiser, Roiss), Lingua franca English or international English as a target language for translation (Snell-Hornby; Orel Kos; Kovacic), and translation teaching and L2 translation (Wussler, Mackenzie and Vienne, Koberski, Pedersen) to the importance of decision-making and confidence for translation teaching and practice (Kralová). Grosman argues that translation is a central instrument of intercultural communication. The impact of translated works in a dominant receiving culture, according to him, is often perceived as negative. In conclusion, he states that non-mother tongue translation from less-widely disseminated languages could help preserve cultural diversity. Similarly, Pokorn argues that the advantage of fluency in the target language that TL natives have can often be counterbalanced by their insufficient knowledge of the source culture or source language, so L1 translation is not automatically superior to L2 translation. In his study, Dollerup talks about the score of proficiency in a target language on a scale. When dealing specifically with the translation of literary texts, he argues that shortcomings of the non-native speaker translator are obvious, because reading literature is an aesthetic experience and only those speakers who move within the 90–100 per cent of the fluency spectrum can reach this level of stylistic perfection. One could argue, just as well, that stylistic perfection is an idealized view of style, and fails to account for style as an idiosyncratic feature of translation and literature.[8] The idea

---

[8] I loosely reference here the 1993 study by Johnson & Rosano, with the key takeaway that 'native English speakers scored better than ESL students on academic measures of English proficiency, but there were no group differences on level of cognitive sophistication in English metaphor interpretation or on a measure of metaphor fluency (number of metaphor interpretations produced)' (1993:159). More specifically, on style within Translation Studies, see Boase-Beier (2006), Mona Baker (2000), among others.

of 100 per cent fluency can also be argued against. Among the existing L2 Translation Studies, it is possible to see a general refusal of this ideal of fluency and style.

All the studies found in Grosman et al. (2000) therefore conclude that translation teaching should include L2 translation because it is a reality, especially in settings of less-widely diffused languages. The reality of the profession calls for better training in specific skills for translation into a non-mother tongue, and this training will provide a necessary base for the practice. Therefore, the mother tongue of the translator is not as important as sufficient and holistic training in different directions of translation, and fluency in genre-specific styles is more important than fluency in the language in general. The majority of the studies in the collection point to the positive outcome of L2 translation teaching activities, and thus to a positive outcome for L2 translation carried out by properly trained professionals and users of the languages in question. It is also a trend within all the studies mentioned that the specific translational context is the key to analysing translation performance.

Saber Zahedi, in the article 'L2 Translation at the Periphery: A Meta-Analysis of Current Views on Translation Directionality' (2013), puts forward a review of literature around the topic of L2 translation. Carrying out such a review is often seen in studies which deal with the topic of L2 translation, which is lacking in theorization and is, in general, excluded from translation theory. What is most interesting in this is how he differentiates between implicit and explicit views on translation directionality. It is Zahedi's aim to show how implicit views that can be found in the scholarly literature about translation have created L1 translation as the norm. Zahedi (2013), Pokorn (2005), and Beeby (1998) are some of the L2 translation scholars who provide an overview of how L2 translation has been received in texts dealing with theorizing translation, both before and after the advent of Translation Studies as a discipline. They divide these assumptions around L2 translation into explicit and implicit. The explicit views are usually found in recent Translation Studies texts, where an author may completely disregard or deny the worth of translating into a non-mother tongue. The implicit views are usually seen in older translation theory, and hint at a preference for L1 translation, thus making the reading audience internalize the idea that translation should ideally be carried out from a L2 into a L1. This distinction proves useful to see how ingrained these ideas are in our thinking about the practice of translation. Therefore, I chose to adopt the division between explicit and implicit ideas proposed by Zahedi, and expand them with other examples, which I will explore in the following section.

Implicit Views on Translation Directionality

Translation paratexts or commentary are early forms of translation theory. Key discussions on word-for-word or sense-for-sense translation include Cicero's ideas on rhetorical translation, St Jerome's Letter to Pammachius, and Bruni's De interpretatione recta. During the Renaissance, Leonardo Bruni stated that a translator must deeply understand both the source and target languages through extensive reading and mastery (Bruni apud Lefevere, 1992:83). Similarly, Erasmus believed that perfect translation from Greek to Latin required a translator to be highly knowledgeable in both languages (Erasmus, 1992:60). Early translation treatises did not emphasize 'natural' fluency but rather a learned proficiency in languages. The concept of a national language or native-speakerism was nascent, with no preference for the mother tongue.

However, seventeenth-century English poet John Dryden asserted that a translator must master both the author's language and their own (Dryden, 1992:104). In the late eighteenth century, Johann Gottfried Herder emphasized adapting words and expressions from a more developed language to one's *mother tongue* (Herder, 1992:74).

Modern views on translation increasingly stress the importance of one's 'own language'. Victor Hugo claimed that translating a foreign writer adds to national poetry (Hugo, 1992:18), and Goethe stated that every translator is a prophet among their own people (Goethe, 1992:25). Friedrich Schleiermacher, in his essay On the Different Methods of Translating (1813), used terms like 'own language' versus 'foreign' language, showing that these authors assumed an L2-L1 direction, or, at least an overall Foreign (2)-Domestic (1) directionality.

Theorization about translation shifted from valuing proficiency in multiple languages to emphasising translating into one's national language for a domestic readership. This shift occurred around the eighteenth to nineteenth century, influencing attitudes towards L2 translation. This section historically surveyed translation directionality and the evolving link between language and nation, demonstrating that the ideas of national language and L1 translation norms are more recent and arbitrary than assumed.

Explicit Views on Translation Directionality: The Perfect Idealized Bilingual Translator

The L1 translation norm is explicit in some writings and implicit in many others. The way these implicit claims deny the value of L2 translation is largely through ignoring the practice altogether, and only when criticizing or comparing the translator's ability in their 'own language' and the 'foreign language' can these ideas be seen. Pokorn (2005) argues:

> The most common approach to the problem of directionality in translation theory is, however, a silent acceptance of the 'traditional' conviction of the necessity to translate into one's mother tongue. Most translation theoreticians do not discuss openly the possibility of choosing one's TL in translation; however, they do covertly express their conviction that only translation into one's mother tongue guarantees a good translation. (Pokorn 2005:30)

Here, Pokorn touches on the element of choice, which is central to the exophonic principle, going beyond assumptions of what languages a translator works best with, or the best/more traditional direction of translation. The assumptions made when thinking about directionality and when defining a good translator/translation are based on the idea of the infallibility of the native speaker, and of a perfectly bilingual translator. Such an idealized translator is always the inferred translator in these theories. At the same time, if a translator is a perfect bilingual, then directionality would not be an issue. Furthermore, we will explore the issue of bilingualism and bilanguaging, and it will become clearer how the idealized perfect bilingual of translation theory does not hold water. Some Translation Studies scholars, such as Anthony Pym, have discussed at length on defining translation competence, translation teaching, and the tendency of Translation Studies to rely on an idealized translator, in his defence of a minimalist approach to translation competence (Pym, 2003). Pym also questioned the concept of the ideal translator often involved in discussions around translation expertise (Pym, 1996). In a defence of a translator-centred view of translation, Zaliwska-Okrutna (2008) postulates that 'since translation involves human minds, real or ideated, but not idealized, the theory of translation cannot confidently depend on postulates and requirements for an ideal translator or ideal translation, with no provisions made for individual mistakes, lack of skill or expertise' (2008:111).

Linguists such as Sydney Lamb also pointed out that each individual's cognitive system is unique and that understanding these systems must consider the real individual and not the ideal one (Lamb, 1992:26). An idealized translator also reflects an idealized view of fluency. This unrealistic view of fluency and the status of languages in the translator's mind makes it harder to understand translation in non-hegemonic contexts. Such a point of view is somewhat detached from the reality of translation – it fails to hold its truth in the real world. Translation is happening every day, every hour, carried out by native and non-native speakers alike, and so the practice is not exclusive to the context of the perfect bilingual. In fact, according to Pokorn, *'since the claim that native speakers have an infallible ability to distinguish native speakers from non-native speakers used to pass unchallenged in applied linguistics, the majority of translation theorists accepted it and consequently demanded that texts be translated only into the translator's mother tongue'* (Pokorn 2005:114).

The issue with the idealized translator or native speaker who always, infallibly, is capable of distinguishing nativeness and naturalness in a target text is also raised by Meta Grosman (2000). Such an issue highlights the correlated issue of whom the translation is being done for, and why naturalness is so desirable, which are also constant debates in Translation Studies in general. One important thing to notice, however, is that a translation can and might not be focused solely on the target readership. The studies that dismiss the practice of literary L2 translation seem to assume that the target text is all there is to it. On that, Grosman argues:

> This view has been given further support by recent translation studies laying emphasis on the importance of the translator's thorough knowledge of the target culture as prerequisite for translations that can really function in the target culture in accordance with the commonly accepted opinion that translations belong to a target culture only. (...) Native speakers involved in translating, on the other hand, are assumed automatically to be highly proficient in their language and well acquainted with their own culture. (Grosman, 2000:21)

This view is closely related to the idea of native-speaker authority, or native-speakerism, assuming that native speakers are inherently better at their native language than a second language speaker. Such a view is very common in those studies that assume a directionality and a perfect bilingual subject, and which deny the variety of proficiency among speakers of any language, and more strongly, genre- and context-specific proficiency. Many Translation Studies scholars have dismissed the practice of L2 translation on the grounds that it does not sound natural, or that the results fail to read like a native text. These scholars, however, do not offer a definition of nativeness in the use of a language or in the interpretation of a text.[9] That seems to be the problem with many theorists who claim the unacceptability of the practice. Pokorn criticizes this lack of definition when she concludes that

> [s]ince the supporters of native superiority do not define the concept of the native speaker, despite the central position they grant to this notion in their theoretical works, their categorical claims seem more than suspect. They do not provide in support of their views any proofs concerning the greater competence and proficiency of native speakers compared to those of near-native speakers and they often ignore or downgrade the possibility of translation pairs, consisting of a native and a non-native speaker of the TL. (Pokorn, 2005:27)

---

[9] For more detailed overviews, see Beeby (1998/2009), Zahedi (2013), Pavlović (2007), and Pokorn (2005).

In a pivotal thesis on the topic, Pavlović (2007) opens with a statement which helps us to see the researcher's stance:

> The author of this study had been a translator working into and out of her second language (L2), English, and L2 translation teacher for more than a decade before finding out about the 'golden rule' followed by translators in major-language settings: You are only ever supposed to work into your first language. The direction of translation that for her and her colleagues was nothing out of the ordinary turned out to be 'inverse', wrong, forbidden. This realization was intriguing, spurring the author's initial interest in directionality as a research topic. A questionnaire survey was conducted, which showed that more than 70% of full-time translators and interpreters in Croatia do more than half of their workload into their L2 English (Pavlović, forthcoming). In many other settings around the world that involved a 'language of limited diffusion', researchers seemed to be describing similar situations. Clearly, what was unthinkable for some translators was everyday practice for others. (Pavlović, 2007:1)

Coming back to Pokorn, it is this golden rule which kept translation scholars from openly recognizing and encouraging the practice of L2 translation. It is also the rule responsible for the lack of theories and studies focusing on this specific type of translation. These ideas assume an idealized native speaker, as well as a perfect bilingual subject. In fact, Pokorn focuses on these assumptions and their failure to connect with reality. Before introducing the problematic of the perfect bilingual, she concludes, on the topic of an ideal native speaker, that

> [s]ome contemporary translation practitioners and theoreticians then uncritically accept the concept of an ideal native speaker as an arbiter and model of grammaticality, who masters his/her mother tongue completely and in all its details, who has access to all the hidden channels of unutterable associative connectedness between words and concepts, and can therefore also create linguistically and culturally impeccable translations. This theoretical position, however, also has an additional corollary: it ethnocentrically defends the notion of the superiority of the 'natural native speaker', the innate state that can never be acquired, and thus rejects the marginal and peripheral (i.e., translators from immigrant communities and the practice of team translation) as necessarily inferior. (Pokorn, 2005:27)

These assumptions of idealized linguistic subjects as L1 translators are not explicitly expressed in Translation Studies. One can see from the very beginning of the discipline that translators have been increasingly asked to be more perfectly bi- or multilingual and multicultural subjects. In his seminal work on the linguistics of translation, Catford claims that 'discovery of textual equivalents is based on the competent bilingual informant or translator' (Catford, 1965:27). That is, he does not define this informant/translator as perfect, but as a *competent* bilingual who can identify equivalencies in translation.

In contemporary Translation Studies, the ideal(ized) translator is a bi- or multicultural subject. For Gutt (1990) and Bell (1991), for example, the translator is not only bi*lingual* but also bi*cultural*, cross-culturally competent in both language in general and specific communicative skills. This trend has continued in more recent theories of translation, such as with the Cultural Turn in Translation Studies, identified/inaugurated by Bassnett and Lefevere (1998), who idealize a high degree of expertise in both cultures involved in the act of translation. This demand for expertise by the translator not only extends to linguistic and cultural knowledge but also to a knowledge of various fields, registers, and discourses (Neubert & Shreve, 1992; Snell-Hornby, 1992; Cao, 1996). In Skopos theory, according to Vermeer (1978), whether such an idealized bilingual and multicultural subject exists is irrelevant. Even if directionality is not openly regarded as an issue (perhaps because it is not an issue at all), would this theory contradict the dominant trend of the L1 translation norm? After all, if the skopos is fulfilled, the direction of translation does not seem to pose a problem, or at least it is not important from this theoretical viewpoint. Twisting the core of the L1 translation norm, if we take Christiane Nord's proposition that 'the translator might not even belong to the addressed audience or the addressed culture' (Nord, 2011:24) when performing L1 translation, and this is seen by the scholar as a 'drawback', then couldn't we argue that L2 translation works best precisely because the translator is part of the intended audience of the source text?

The rule against L2 translation generally hinges on 'naturalness' and 'authenticity'. Scholars like Newmark (1988), Samuelsson-Brown (1995), Chesterman (2004), and Duff (1989) view L2 translation as unnatural, often blaming native language interference. Newmark, in his *Textbook of Translation*, states: 'Translating into your language of habitual use is the only way you can translate naturally and accurately and with maximum effectiveness' (Newmark, 1988:3), thus suggesting L2 translators produce unnatural outputs. He avoids using 'native speaker' or 'mother tongue', but scholars like Zahedi argue that these claims lack objective data, and show a clear bias (Zahedi, 2013:45).

Marmaridou (1996) examines directionality through cognitive linguistics. She finds that translation into a L1 yields better results, with L2 translations being more sign-oriented than sense-oriented. However, her study is flawed as it disallowed dictionary use, which does not reflect real-world translation (Marmaridou, 1996:50). Translation competence, as noted by Pym (2003), involves more than just lexical knowledge; it includes problem-solving and extra-linguistic skills. David Bellos, in turn, offers a more positive view on L2 translation, emphasizing the translator's comfort with the target language over native status (Bellos, 2016:63–64). Some scholars, like Michael Cronin in

Translation and Identity (2006), do not explicitly address directionality, but use less-loaded phrases, avoiding 'natural', 'own', and 'mother tongue', for example. Lawrence Venuti (1998), despite advocating for foreignizing translation, does not discuss the translator's mother tongue, indicating a possible openness to L2 translation (Pokorn, 2005:33).

Studies outside the European/Western context are emerging. Wang (2009, 2011) highlights China's policy of outward translation by preferring native Chinese translators. In the Arabic context, Jamoussi (2015) discusses L2 translation as essential for cultural export. Di Giovanni & Dirar (2015) examine directionality in African translation history, focusing on missionary activities. They reference Bandia's distinction between horizontal pre-colonial, and vertical colonial translation practices, noting the ideological basis of colonial translations. These recent studies indicate a growing academic interest in directionality. However, the field of L2 translation remains underdeveloped, with many norms against it based on unproven claims, even with historical evidence showing that L2 translation was more common than often assumed.

Directionality in Translation Process Research

In the field of translation process research (TPR), there has been an attempt to study directionality by empirical means. Translation process research is a subfield of Translation Studies which deals with the cognitive processing of translation, and uses research tools such as key-logging, eye-tracking, think-aloud protocols, machine translation, and even, in some cases, fMRI screening. Often, TPR triangulates data collected through these tools with other interdisciplinary data, such as cognitive tests (e.g. working memory), textual analyses, surveys/questionnaires, among others. Topics that are highlighted and prioritized in this subarea include the differences between novice and expert translators, time and structural constraints, and decision-making and problem-solving. Directionality is also a topic that can be found in such studies. The neutral way in which directionality is often tested in TPR also means that, in most cases, there is no value judgement on which directionality is better. Maybe Literary Translation Studies could take a leaf out of TPR's book and study directionality with a more neutral outlook, seen as a reality and a field for empirical work, for testing hypotheses rather than making general, unbacked claims. The present work is not within TPR. However, it is with a short overview of L2 translation and directionality studies within the area of TPR that I aim to show how such a practice can be seen explicitly in a more balanced light.

By and large TPR that deals with directionality does so with the aim of testing potential differences in the translation process between different directionalities, not deciding on which direction is the better one. A value judgement between groups or participants is not usually the goal of empirical endeavours, but it is important to point out that most of these studies exist precisely because different translation directionalities are a reality of the profession, something that the L1 translation norm ignores. Directionality studies within TPR, by focusing on cognitive data, are more preoccupied with understanding the different cognitive paths, loads, and strategies involved in translating into different directions. Similarly to what happens in Bilingual research, directionality in TPR is tested empirically to understand where the differences, if any, lie. As is usual in this type of research, an important attribute to separating the groups under scrutiny is experience: experts versus novice translators. Some studies, like Whyatt (2019), concluded that text type had more of an impact on task time than directionality, but that, overall, the latter did not have a statistically significant effect on task time. According to the author, 'Directionality effects interplay with text-type effects, and possibly with the translators' individual experience and working style' (Whyatt, 2019:94). Whyatt's findings diverge from other similar studies in the area, such as Buchweitz & Alves (2006), according to whom

> [t]ranslating from the first language into the second language (Pt-Eng) required timewise approximately 30 percent more of the translators in this study. Hence, it slowed down their rhythm. This result is relevant not only for an academically oriented (or educationally) discussion of translation. It is likewise important for learning the ropes of the profession, considering that time, in terms of deadlines, is a very valuable commodity for the job of the translator. (Buchweitz & Alves, 2006:251–252)

However, as Whyatt contends: 'The difference in the findings can be explained by many factors, including the number of participants, language-pair specificity and the length or intensity of professional experience in providing L1 → L2 translation' (2019:94). And, in fact, other studies in TPR reached similar results to those of Whyatt (da Silva et al., 2017). Revisiting Buchweitz & Alves, the issue of time and effort in translation, even though vital for technical translators, has different implications for literary translators. Deadlines exist and do govern the work of literary translators. However, literary translation jobs arguably have longer timelines, making strict deadlines and daily wordcount less influential.

Most TPR dealing with directionality aims to test task time and cognitive effort, some with noticeable differences between what TPR researchers call DT (direct translation) and IT (inverse translation), L1 and L2 translation, respectively. Even for those studies which concluded that there was a significant time deficit in the L1-L2 direction compared to L2-L1, with reservations, one could argue that the agent affected in this transaction would be the translator, not the final text. For example, Stasimioti et al. (2021) found that L2-L1 was less demanding than L1-L2, but that directionality did not imply differences in quality. Interestingly, research has shown that directionality also impacts other cognitive aspects. For example, Jia et al. (2023) found that directionality significantly affects translator anxiety levels, influencing cognitive load and task processing. Additionally, studies by Pietryga (2022) indicate that students perceive L2 translation as more cognitively demanding and challenging, especially regarding vocabulary and terminology, although these preferences may evolve with training. Is this anxiety influenced by the L1 translation norm? As the study shows, this anxiety affects cognitive load, so going against what is considered natural in translation directionality may cause the difficulties relevant to said directionality. In many of these studies, the conclusion is that more research on the topic is needed, as well as the caveat that such conclusions are limited and influenced by many factors, such as the idiosyncrasies of the translators involved and of specific language combinations. According to Ferreira & Schwieter:

> As the number of studies in translation process research and, most specifically, cognitive translation process research increases, scholars must soon offer more contributions to directionality in translation and shed light on IT specificities as a consequence of its high demand throughout the world. Future work must not forget cultural and identity aspects of the translator as they most certainly shape TT construction. For decades, translation process research has borrowed from theories and methodologies from other disciplines, yet IT has received limited attention. We are optimistic that this interest will change in the very near future. (Ferreira & Schwieter, 2017:102)

There is, however, one last topic to heed upon concluding this section. That is, the fact that in the literature of TPR studies dealing with directionality, once again, most of this work has been carried out and written in English, by non-native speakers of English, in countries that do not have English as one of their official languages: Whyatt's (2019) and Pietryga's (2022) work in Poland; Pavlović's in Slovenia; Buchweitz & Alves (2006), Ferreira (2013, 2014), and Fonseca (2014) in Brazil; Wang (2009, 2011), Chang & Chen (2023), and Jia et al. (2023) in China; Stasimioti et al. (2021) in Greece; Shin (2021) in Korea; Hagemann (2019) in Germany; and Malkiel (2004) in Israel; among several others spread around the globe. Directionality being studied and described through exophonic writing seems to be a tried and tested reality in many contexts.

Summation

The scholars whose studies were reviewed in the first part of this section all agree on one issue: that directionality is often invisible, ignored by Translation Studies at large. The very fact that a gathering of opinions and studies on directionality in this area does not yield a sufficient number of results and that most of these call for more studies is telling of the current status of L2 translation within Translation Studies. In many cases, the term which draws these studies together is directionality, as there are many differing views on which other terms to use: L2 translation, A-B translation, IT, non-native translation, and so on. A cornerstone in the L1 translation norm is that a translator's relationship with language is fixed and unchanging. Alongside relationship with language, we can add translation competence and second language fluency, which are also not fixed, nor unchanging. As Trainor puts it:

> Although the question of whether a translator is born or made is still a matter of debate, few doubt that practice is the key to improvement in a variety of fields, and translation is no exception. Just as written expression techniques can be acquired, we are convinced that we can also acquire skills to improve our ability to translate, even into a second language. (Cruz Trainor, 2004:60)[10]

This begs the question, once again, of who benefits from dogmas such as the L1 translation norm. In what way would Translation Studies be weakened or severely affected as a discipline by allowing translators to translate into a second language or be trained in it. Questions such as these have yet to be answered, and the answer may lie in (1) a greater dialogue between the many areas within the discipline of Translation Studies, which often do not benefit from an exchange between themselves (and thus remain monodisciplinary in an inherently interdisciplinary area), (2) a closer look at the foundations of such monological tenets, and (3) looking at L2 translators as the agents, and not at the translated text, to understand how they see their practice.

2 Monolingual, Multilingual, and Exophonic

Monophones and Mother Tongues: Creating the Native

> Proficiency in the adopted language alone decided whether integration was accomplished or not, a measuring stick that perpetuated and reinvented the migrants' outsider status; their foreignness, the accent, oral or written, betrayed

---

[10] 'Aunque la pregunta de si el traductor nace o se hace sigue siendo objeto de debate, pocos ponen en duda que la práctica es clave para mejorar en diversidad de ámbitos y la traducción no es una excepción. Al igual que se pueden adquirir técnicas de expresión escrita, estamos convencidos de que también podemos adquirir destrezas para mejorar nuestra habilidad para traducir, incluso a una segunda lengua.' All translations are my own, unless otherwise noted.

all confidence of belonging and served as an instrument of exclusion. . . .seen in this light, the foreign language can be perceived as monolithic, immutable and sacrosanct, the standard language as a system of exclusion and the scrupulous mastery of it as an impossible ideal, a Sisyphean undertaking. (Stoklosinski, 2014:20)

The first part of this section will concern itself with the coming-of-age of the monolingual ideal. This contrasts with the second part, which will deal with all that is multiple and all that defies monolingual and monocultural ideals. With Yildiz's (2012) proposition of a post-monolingual paradigm, we follow onto less monotopic views of language. The aim of this section is to show both the charged history of these concepts surrounding languages and their recency. These concepts may also serve certain viewpoints that do not take the plurality of language practices into consideration. My argument here is that translation should no longer uphold such outdated values.

Monolinguistic Ethnocentrism and Monolingual Myths

When talking about nation and language, it is of great importance to discuss the idea of the mother tongue and monolingualism in general. Scholars have proved that in medieval and early modern times translation was much more visible and carried out from one language to the other without necessarily demanding from the translator a mother tongue ability of the target language. It can also be said that in these times, in fact, multilingualism was much more present in the writing of literature, and to test the limits of poetic language in different mediums. The assumption that the world is largely made up of separate and different monolingual communities is what scholars who deal with multilingualism call the monolingual bias (or monolingual *habitus*).[11] Monolingualism is a much more recent phenomenon, and if we start from a Western-European, Anglophone school of thought, we might err in thinking that the world is so much more simple and monolingual than it actually is.

Contemporary sociolinguistics, especially the study of multilingualism, strive to move away from monoglot Eurocentric definitions of language and deconstruct these perspectives which are based on the monolingual. According to Love (2009), the monolingual culture that pervades linguistic discourse is 'an exercise in culture maintenance' (2009:31). This culture maintenance also comes in the form of inventing languages, grammar, and seeing language through a linguist perspective: that of language as

---

[11] I will explore the concept of *habitus* in depth in Section 3.

a monolith.¹² As Benedict Anderson proposed that nations are imagined communities, linguists such as Alastair Pennycook and David Gramling propose that languages are also not only imagined but also invented, the result of a conscious project to standardize and separate languages from dialects. More recently, from the 1970s onwards, some scholars, such as Einar Haugen, who created the concept of language ecology, claimed such fixed concepts to be altogether false. According to him, 'the concept of language as a rigid, monolithic structure is false, even if it has proved to be a useful fiction in the development of languages. It is the kind of simplification that is necessary at a certain stage of a science, but which can now be replaced by more sophisticated models' (Haugen, 1972:325).

Then, if we have moved past the need for a rigid view of a language as a single entity, what do we have? Firstly, it is necessary to understand not only how the old views came to be but also how pervasive such an idea was on different levels of language thought. According to Makoni and Pennycook (2006), not only were languages invented, so too were conceptions of languageness and metalanguage.¹³ The notion of language as a separate entity has been proven by linguists across different continents to be invented (see Harries, 1987; Heryanto 1995; Mannheim, 1991; Kuzar, 2001 among others). The drive to test this notion and disprove it arises when scholars noticed how the monological approach to languages failed to understand their use in context. Not all people belonging to different language communities have one or two or more languages, thought of as such, as independent bounded entities that form a set of linguistic assets, as is often assumed in Anglo or Eurocentric thought (Heryanto, 1990). In fact, such meta-discursive regimes (Bauman and Briggs, 2003) have hindered the study of multilingualism in the linguistic realities of former colonies and of complex linguistic contexts beyond the Western European? Language contact and its subsequent many dialects, creoles, and variants proved that well-defined linguistic monoliths such as national languages did not capture accurately the linguistic realities of these communities. These linguistic structures were 'responses to discourse needs' (Bybee and Hopper, 2001:2) in that in seeing languages as objects one could also more easily categorize, master, and control such fictitious

---

¹² According to David Gramling, Lingualism is 'a term invoked occasionally in Usage-Based Linguistics to critique the premise or belief, that languages are essentially coherent, stable, nameable entities that people can master and possess' (Gramling 2021:27). From this point onwards I will choose to call attitudes and views that follow a lingualism perspective as 'lingualist', the adjective for lingualism.

¹³ Languageness is Dorotskar's (2014) translation equivalent of *Sprachigkeit*, meaning all forms of proficiency, spread and use of language (2014:389). However, in sociolinguistics, this is defined as that which defines a language, self-identification, and social group's beliefs being central to defining what constitutes a language (cf. Tosco, 2021).

entities. With these, linguistic gatekeeping could be created, a highly racialized feature of language policing and language control. But the innate instinct to protect languages as entities came to be as a result of the attempt to categorize and control languages in order to study them. Grammar has always been seen as a fixed entity, a set of unchanging and unchangeable rules of a language, but scholars such as Hopper (1998) proposed the idea of grammar as emergent, as temporary, dependent on repeated social activity.

Language loyalty and language awareness are rather recent creations in the history of human thought. Seeing languages as separate, bounded entities and not within their context of use would mean also ignoring the fundamental social notions of community and humanity, central to language anthropology (Kroskrity 2000; Woolard, 2002). Such a notion did not exist in pre-colonial times. In fact, prior to colonial encounters, the differences between varieties of language use had different meanings in colonial settings (Pennycook & Makoni, 2012). As David Gramling states in his book *The Invention of Monolingualism* (2018), 'indigenous people in the colonies were gradually de-competenced through a multilingual process of monolingualisation' (2018:15). Monolingualism was forced upon these colonized populations, and the European languages established in these colonies were artificial implantations, and their colonized users merely suboptimal users of the language. Their natural multilingualism was erased in favour of a colonial language. This resulted in 'an undeniable reality – namely, that colonialism has profound consequences on colonised subjects as linguistic or language subjects; that at the core of the colonial enterprise, whether by systemic design or not, is an active production of subjection through the discipline of language' (Chow, 2014:37).

This monolingual bias so prevalent in our episteme, used as the norm for language research, literary studies, and Translation Studies, greatly affects communities and language users who do not fit these strict categories. In fact, the very concept of the native speaker as well as that of a mother tongue are creations of the same discursive practice of the monolingual imaginary.[14] In the following section, I will explore some monolingually inclined concepts and how they relate to each other.

Mother Tongues and the Language Family Romance

The term 'mother tongue' has a complex history, particularly in a context where traditional roles of women and mothers are being analysed and increasingly

---

[14] Antonio Esposito (1995) denounced the medieval monolingual imaginary present in language, philology, and, I would add, also present in translation.

questioned. Bonfiglio (2010) provides an overview of its developments. Traditionally, 'mother tongue' is seen as a calque of medieval Latin's 'lingua materna', from the Catholic church's Latin use in the Middle Ages. Some German scholars argued it originates from the German 'Muttersprache', but Spitzer (1942) provides evidence of earlier occurrences in Romance languages, cementing it as a medieval Catholic neologism. Bonfiglio cites iconography showing the Virgin Mary breastfeeding Jesus, linking this to language nurturing (Bynum, 1986). Dante Alighieri's 'De vulgari eloquentia' (1304) helped cement the idea of mother tongue versus Latin, using nurturing metaphors. He first uses 'maternam locutionem' in Latin, positioning vernacular as natural and Latin as artificial. Renaissance scholars reinforced this image, connecting mammary metaphors to language power (Bonfiglio, 2013). As a result of the 100-Years War, In England, English had to assert its supremacy against French, often using gendered attributions. Davidson (2009) claims English was constructed as superior to French in the post-medieval period, seen as a manly language opposed to the feminine French. In a trilingual England (French, Latin, and English), post-100 Years War, a divide between English and French led to efforts to erase multilingualism from English history, framing French as foreign (Butterfield, 2009). English became the national language, relegating other languages to the home. This monolingual public versus multilingual private sphere explains current multilingualism approaches in language policy, notably in post-Brexit UK.

The mother tongue remains a potent metaphor in literary writing, tying to monolingual ideals and the family romance model, defined by Yildiz (2012) as affective ties to languages, further complicating linguistic relationships. The myths of the native speaker and mother tongue remain powerful and uncontested. Gilmour (2020) states their power lies in their ubiquity and authority over language authenticity (Gilmour, 2020:101). If we want to contest such terms, we must look to those, like Chow, who aim to do exactly that, and propose new ways and new paradigms to counter the powerful myths of the mother tongue and the native speaker. Hopefully, this Element will show how fraught this view of language-as-monolith can be when applied to translation, and to L2 translation in particular.

On the Strength of Native-Speakerism

The monolingual bias assumes that languages are discrete and that users are inherently monolingual, even when considering multilingualism as multiple monolingualisms. A critical term here is the native speaker, an idealized monoglot construct that does not hold up under scrutiny. Claire Kramsch notes:

> The only speech community traditionally recognized by foreign language departments has been the middle-class, ethnically dominant male citizenry of nation-states, as Mary-Louise Pratt argues. The native speaker is in fact an imaginary construct – a canonically literate monolingual middle-class member of a largely fictional national community whose citizens share a belief in a common history and a common destiny (...). And this ideal corresponds less and less to reality. (Kramsch, 2003:255)

This construct of the native speaker perpetuates myths in linguistics and literature. Holliday (2006) introduced 'native-speakerism' to address this pervasive myth. Damian Rivers traces the term's origin to an 1858 lecture by George P. Marsh, who advocated for English philology in American curricula, emphasizing language homogeneity. Rivers explains Marsh's viewpoint:

> One can make connections between beliefs concerning language ownership, the maintenance of language standards and the relationship between language nativity and race, in addition to the role of language in national identity, all derived from the position that 'languages adhere so tenaciously to their native soil, that, in general, they can be eradicated only by the extirpation of the races that speak them'. (Marsh, 1859:88) (Rivers, 2018:18)

Scholars link the native speaker concept to race and nativity, criticized in raciolinguistics (Cameron, 2007; Alim, 2016; Aneja, 2016; Rosa & Flores, 2017). Sociolinguistics evidence suggests native speakers do not always outperform non-natives linguistically (Hulstjin, 2015). Kramsch (2003) highlights that native speakers often exhibit diverse linguistic variations, challenging the unitary native speaker notion. Treffers-Daller (2018) supports this by showing that native speaker abilities vary widely:

> Comparing L2 learners with presumably monolingual native speakers is also problematic because such native speakers' abilities differ widely from each other. Alderson (1980) not only found that what he termed native speakers did not always restore grammatical gaps in a cloze test but also that the differences between native and what he called non-native (L2) speakers were very small, and that some non-native speakers outperformed the native ones. These findings led Alderson to conclude that 'native speaker proficiency, even on lower-order tasks, varies' (p. 74), and he considered the use of native speakers as criteria-setting for non-native speakers on tests 'misguided' (p. 75). In a similar vein, Hamilton et al. (1993) reported on the performance of presumably

monolingual native speakers on a reading and writing test that is widely used with adults seeking to work or study in an English-speaking country (the International English Language Testing System, IELTS; see www.ielts.org/). Hamilton et al. found this performance 'far from homogeneous'. (p. 348) (Treffers-Daller, 2018:290)

Given this variability, using native speakers as benchmarks is questionable. In language teaching, there is a call for a 'post-native-speakerist pedagogy' (Holliday, 2006; Houghton & Hashimoto, 2018). Could there be a similar call for a post-native-speakerist Translation Studies?

Despite practical arguments for a native speaker model, it is essential to critique this homogenous norm. Raciolinguists and postcolonialists criticise the racist implications of assumed nativity. Chow states:

> Can anyone ever be expected to inhabit discourse archives as a native speaker, whose enunciations are permanently free of the interference of other forms of speaking and writing? Should not the idea of the native speaker as such – a putative sovereign subject and author, imagined to be in full possession of her language and at one with her own speaking voice – be recognized as a last bastion of those epistemic unities that, as Foucault shows, are emblematic of the long-standing practices of knowledge production based on the exclusion of discontinuity? (Chow, 2014:56–57)

Chow challenges the native speaker's neutrality, emphasizing that what is excluded is labelled an exception, not the outdated norm itself. On non-nativeness as a symptom of discontinuity, she concludes:

> Because the native speaker is thought to occupy an uncorrupted origination point, learning a language as a non-native speaker can only be an exercise in woeful approximation. The failure to sound completely like the native speaker is thus given a pejorative name: '(foreign) accent'. Having an accent is, in other words, the symptom precisely of discontinuity – an incomplete assimilation, a botched attempt at eliminating another tongue's competing copresence. In geopolitical terms, having an accent is tantamount to leaving on display – rather than successfully covering up – the embarrassing evidence of one's alien origins and migratory status. (Think, for instance, of Derrida's unease at not being entirely rid of his Algerian accent on some occasions.) The speech of the native speaker, in contrast, is deemed so natural that it is said to be without – or shall we say outside? – an accent. (Chow, 2014:58)

Chow proposes a 'xenophone' language domain, resisting the native speaker model and embracing linguistic plurality. While not yet adopted widely, it aligns with L2 translation as an exophonic practice. Exploring the myths of language nativity, such as the mother tongue and family romance, will further clarify these issues.

The Post-monolingual Condition

Yasemin Yildiz, in her book *Beyond the Mother Tongue* (2012), also offers an analysis of multi- and monolingualism from a historical approach. According to the author, monolingualism is a relatively recent phenomenon, but a highly successful one, aided and based on a monolingual paradigm that obscured from view the multilingual nature of Europe both in the present but also in the past. It is believed that this paradigm had its onset at the end of the eighteenth century.[15] The monolingual bias and monolingual *habitus* of our modern way of thinking affect the construction of individuals and their proper subjectivity, the formation of disciplines and institutions, and imagined collectives, culminating in a most base/essential sense in cultures and nations.

But what is the post-monolingual paradigm? This term, introduced by the author, uses the prefix 'post' in a historicizing approach as temporally dominated, that is, it signifies the period since the emergence of monolingualism as the dominant paradigm, which first occurred in late eighteenth-century Europe. (Yildiz, 2012:4). This paradigm, however, spread in different ways across varied contexts, so the term would also need a more flexible character in order to define the period or the paradigm both temporally after monolingualism as a dominant ideal, but also the tension between mono- and multilingual contexts. In this sense, according to Yildiz, the post-monolingual paradigm 'refers to the unfolding of the effects of the monolingual and not to its successful overcoming or transcendence' (Yildiz, 2012:4). It offers, at the same time, with 'post', a critical function to the dominance of the monolingual *habitus*, a struggle against, a rupture. In the author's own words, 'postmonolingual in this study refers to a field of tension in which the monolingual paradigm continues to assert itself and multilingual practices persist or reemerge. This term therefore can bring into sharper focus the back-and-forth movement between these two tendencies that characterizes contemporary linguistic constellations' (Yildiz, 2012:5).

The German context, which is considered to be one of the founding grounds of the monolingual paradigm, also offers nowadays many counteractions to the monolingual bias. In the political turmoil that were the eighteenth and nineteenth centuries, German thinkers such as Herder, Humboldt, Schleiermacher, and Wagner, to name a few, started spreading the romantic notion of a natural language tied to a nation, a people, a *Volk*. According to anthropologist Susan Gal (1993), language started to be seen as an object, with particular attributes, after the romantic reaction to the Enlightenment. Herder saw language as emanating from a particular people. According to Yildiz, 'the multiplication

---

[15] The linguist Einar Haugen (1966) first defined the monolingual bias as likely stemming from historical processes of nation-building and cultural assimilation.

of languages is not an issue for this Herderian view as long as each language is conceived as distinct and separate and as belonging to just one equally distinct and separate people' (Yildiz, 2012:7).

In the chapters that constitute Yildiz's monograph, the author explores several examples of writers in the German-speaking context who are in some way or another negating the monolingual paradigm of German: Franz Kafka, Theodor Adorno, Yoko Tawada, Emine Özdamar, and Feridun Zaimoğlu. She argues that all of these authors see mother tongue in the German context in a different way, be it as a site of alienation, identity, exclusion, inclusion, or violence. These authors do not negate or move against German but rather show how German in their context is different from the public discourse around the homogeneity of the German language. According to Yildiz:

> This stress on homogeneity, I would argue, constitutes an inadvertent admission of the reality of heterogeneity. In post-monolingual terms, it constitutes an attempted reassertion of the monolingual paradigm vis-à-vis the realization of multilingual realities. Coloring the tongue is a response to recognizing that not all tongues are German, that the country is multilingually inhabited. This particular vision does not want to admit the nature of multilingual practices, the ability to live multiple belongings, but neither does it want to admit the reality that many minorities are already German speakers, even if the dominant society does not yet believe that. (Yildiz, 2012:208)

These authors, and in fact others who could be added to this roster, are destabilising the connection once thought inherent and indivisible between language and ethnicity. This connection forgets that it portrays language as a standardized system, rather than as a social and cultural practice. If language is seen as the latter, language as a practice is one of the multiple ways the post-monolingual paradigm proposes its major transgressions. Again, as stated by Yildiz:

> The German that emerges here in postmonolingual perspective has been and continues to be a home for many – a home that is itself undergoing transformation, a home that is not exclusionary, that it is impure, marked, tainted, 'enriched', and charged. The use of German by those not deemed legitimate speakers, whether Kafka or Zaimoğlu, indicates that German is already a lingua franca – with all the de/formations that happen to such a language, as the different forms of 'Englishes' in the world demonstrate. This view of German as a lingua franca rather than as a purely national language could be a curative to the proprietary, exclusionary claims made on the language today. (2012:211)

As we see in this quote, Yildiz raises the issue of German as a lingua franca. The study of the world's lingua francas and its many historical, political, cultural implications is a rich area which looks closely at how national languages become deterritorialized and turn into a global, international language, yet not necessarily culture-free (Hülmbauer et al., 2008; Baker, 2009; Cogo, 2012). English, as the perceived major lingua franca in many contexts, has its own area of studies – English as a Lingua Franca (ELF). There are different perspectives within the area, some arguing that those who speak ELF should not be considered learners, but users, while some criticize the native-speakerism still present in the teaching of EFL. The study of lingua francas is a fast-evolving discipline, due to the very dynamic nature of the objects of study. For this reason, and so as not to expand tangentially in another terminological direction, a mention of lingua franca as a move towards deterritorializing languages will suffice. There is a need for more studies on translation and lingua francas and the many gatekeeping practices in place. For the time being it is important to notice that in a post-monolingual paradigm the connection between language and nation is no longer straightforward. This connection moves away from essential ideas about a language and its natives and into the many ways in which languages in use are changed by different languaging practices.

At this textual crossroads I would like to bring back a provocation from Pokorn's (2005) study to foreground how the themes and topics raised in this section connect to the issue of L2 translation. As she puts it:

> Some contemporary translation practitioners and theoreticians then uncritically accept the concept of an ideal native speaker as an arbiter and model of grammaticality, who masters his/her mother tongue completely and in all its details, who has access to all the hidden channels of unutterable associative connectedness between words and concepts, and can therefore also create linguistically and culturally impeccable translations. This theoretical position, however, also has an additional corollary: it ethnocentrically defends the notion of the superiority of the 'natural native speaker', the innate state that can never be acquired, and thus rejects the marginal and peripheral (i.e. translators from immigrant communities and the practice of team translation) as necessarily inferior. (Pokorn, 2005:27)

As Pokorn eloquently posits, these 'uncritically accepted concepts' must be unpacked, repeatedly, and translation practitioners and theoreticians must come to terms with evolutions in other disciplines regarding these myths which sustain the beliefs still rampant in Translation Studies, especially when talking about literary translation. We must be wary of norms which exclude such a great number of people from the communities of interpretation and action within literary translation. Literary Translation Studies, into English especially, must face various privileges, prejudices, and dangerously excluding practices which are still acting to keep some translation practices, such as L2 translation, as a suboptimal outlier in the translation world.

Bilinguals or Multilinguals?

In this subsection, I will explore key concepts beyond monolingualism – those that try to name and understand when people use more than one language. In this overview, the reader will encounter several terms: bilingual, languaging, bilanguaging, multilingualism, plurilingualism, translingualism, translanguaging, and exophony. There is discussion around the differences between the various terms: both in definition and in application, and I intend to give an overview of the main issues. However, the aim is not to create further confusion, adding another species to this fauna of terminology. The objective here is to foreground the multiplicity of language practices, the inherent monolingual bias even in multilingualism studies and approaches. The studies and issues foregrounded here will also show the epistemic weakness in trying to forcefully tie these concepts down in favour of language order and of a linguistic utopia (Pratt, 1987) still prevalent in Translation Studies.

Bilingualism ands Bilanguaging

When discussing translation, particularly translation directionality or language pairs, two languages are involved: the source language and the target language. In the US, Translation Studies are often situated within Comparative Literature, assuming two languages. In the UK, translation often falls within Modern Languages departments, linked to distinct national languages. Comparative Literature often views multilingualism as multiple monolingualisms. The term 'bilingualism' implies two languages, but how is it defined?

From Bloomfield's (1933) narrow definition of bilingualism as 'the native-like control of two or more languages' to Diebold's (1964) broader incipient bilingualism, the term has been extensively debated. Bilingualism is classified into individual and societal types (Baker, 2001), with dimensions ranging from language ability to use. Stern (1992) noted the lack of standardized terminology in language proficiency, complicating the study of bilingualism. Valdés and Figueroa (1994) categorized bilingualism into age, ability, balance of languages, development, context of acquisition, and elective versus circumstantial bilingualism. These dimensions exceed Bloomfield's definition and consider the classic linguistic skills: listening, speaking, reading, and writing. These skills are not always balanced, as Colin Baker (2001:5) notes, and include sub-scales not easily quantified. Skutnabb-Kangas (1981) added inner thinking as a possible fifth language ability. Baker (2001:6) contrasted maximal and minimal bilingualism definitions by Bloomfield and Diebold.

Bilingualism varies in proficiency levels and language use. Cummins (1984) emphasized academic competence in a language, distinct from native or bilingual speakers' abilities. Bassetti (2012) highlighted the difference between bilinguals and biliterates, crucial in translating written texts. Bassetti noted that spoken language is innate, while written language is learned, affecting sequential bilinguals who may excel in spelling but not pronunciation. This differentiation is central to L2 writing and translation, focusing on language users, not speakers. Chomsky (1965) distinguished between language competence and performance, highlighting the complexities of bilingual performance. The categorization of bilinguals depends on the purpose, often leading to a suppression or maximization of bi- or multilingualism. The ideal of balanced bilingualism is rare, as Fishman (1971) pointed out, questioning the concept of 'equilinguals'.

Government policies, especially in English-speaking countries, often use a monolingual/fractional view, comparing bilingual abilities to monolingual test scores. This view overlooks socioeconomic factors affecting language access and use. Baker noted the monolingual bias despite the prevalence of bilingualism globally (2001:8). Grosjean (1985, 1994) advocated assessing bilinguals' communicative competence rather than traditional language tests, considering their multi-competencies (Cook, 1992). Hansegård's (1975) semilingualism proposition faced criticism for ignoring context and qualitative aspects of language competencies and for being problematic in that it produced an 'unforgiving theory of linguistic pathology directed at minoritized bilinguals in Sweden's far north' (Karlander & Salö, 2023:506). Treffers-Daller (2018) criticized the deficit view comparing bilinguals to monolinguals, which persists in SLA and bilingualism studies despite Skutnabb-Kangas's (1981) warning. Ortega (2013) and Pearson (2010) called for a bi-/multilingual turn in SLA and bilingualism fields, recognizing conversational fluency and academic competence differences. Hernández-Chavez (1978) and Oller & Perkins (1980) proposed specific language proficiency components and global proficiency concepts. Cummins (2000) and Skutnabb-Kangas & Toukomaa (1976) differentiated academic and conversational language proficiency. Fishman's functional bilingualism and language choice, as noted by Baker (2001:13), involve context and degree of contact. Code-switching, studied by Li Wei et al. (1992), is a reality for bilinguals, leading to Baker's conclusion that defining bilingualism is elusive (2001:15).

As we can see, definitions of bilingualism are constantly being updated, challenged, and more complex issues are added to the mix, making it increasingly harder, if not impossible, to see bilingualism outside of specific contexts. Bilingualism as a social phenomenon involves access to linguistic codes for communication, as Hamers & Blanc noted (2000:6). Translators, embodying bilinguality, navigate the complexities of translating between different languages and cultures. Language use is not monolithic but a collection of heterogeneous constructions adapting to contexts (Beeby & Hopper, 2001). The L1 translation norm persists due to traditional Translation Studies' monolingual bias and the monolithic view of language which is still pervasive in the field, despite advances in language study recognizing complex linguistic prisms.

Multilingualism and Plurilingualism: Problems of Definition

In the small and recent body of scholarship on pre-colonial multilingual language practice, another term has been proposed: plurilingualism. Canagarajah & Liyanage (2012) argue that plurilingualism better addresses pre-colonial linguistic realities, especially where it differs from multilingualism. The Language Policy Division of the Council of Europe defines plurilingualism as 'The intrinsic capacity of all speakers to use and learn, alone or through teaching, more than one language' (2000:168). It differs from societal and individual multilingualism: 'Societal multilingualism refers to languages having separate identities in distinct areas. Individual multilingualism refers to separate, advanced competence in the different languages one speaks – almost like separate monolingualisms' (Canagarajah & Liyanage, 2012:50). Plurilingualism implies these language competences are dynamically related. It innovatively reworks language competence as using different languages for distinct purposes, focusing on integrated rather than separate competencies.

Multilingualism can be seen in some contexts as elitist due to societal limitations on multi- and plurilingualism. This perception persists because multilingualism is used as an umbrella term for diverse plurilingual practices, viewing languages and competencies separately through a language-as-commodity lens (cf. Gramling, 2021). Terms like 'acquire' and 'master' reinforce this view. Language is treated as a commodity added to curricula to enhance prospects. However, this privilege is not extended to heritage speakers or those learning languages due to colonial subjugation or migration. Scholars proposing alternative terminologies acknowledge that differentiating multilingual practices may do more harm than good. Canagarajah & Liyanage (2012) state: 'The difference between multilingualism and plurilingualism is largely theoretical. The terms reflect different perceptions of language relationships in society and individual repertoire. Monolingual assumptions in linguistics have skewed the understanding of multilingualism' (Canagarajah & Liyanage, 2012:50).

This distinction aims to provide a new perspective on language practices, free from concepts of homogeneity and uniformity. However, further attempts to categorize multilingualism must consider its inherent instability and diversity. Gramling (2021) argues: 'Those seeking to define multilingual experience for policy may force consensus where none exists. In the coming decades, multilingual experience will become even harder to define, and perhaps it should remain so' (Gramling, 2021:11). How will this difficulty of definition affect Translation Studies?

Language as Performance

The difference between competence and performance was stressed by Chomsky (1965), but even before that, Ferdinand Saussure offered similar binaries with his distinction between *langue* and *parole*. However, for the longest time, language studies have focused solely on competence. Even when these considered performance alongside competence, the former was often put aside, an afterthought (Hymes, 1972). Sociolinguist Alastair Pennycook, when proposing an approach to language as performance, defines it thus:

> What this does, crucially, is challenge the centrality of *competence* (underlying system) over *performance*. Thus, by looking at the performativity of language – how in the doing it does that which it purports to be – we can start to question the foundation of linguistic belief in system, and go beyond mere reporting of performance. Instead, this opens up the space to explore how sedimentation occurs (and can be opposed). More generally, we can start to raise broader questions about the whole ontological status of the notion of language and languages. Languages are no more pre given entities that pre-exist our linguistic performances than are gendered or ethnic identities. Rather they are the sedimented products of repeated acts of identity. (Pennycook, 2004:15)

In this subsection, we will look at discussions on language performativity ranging from the constellation of terms around languaging, ideas around mono- and multilingual drag and passing, and finishing with language as a prosthesis and exophony. These discussions are essential as they challenge fixed ideas about language and open possibilities for language to be seen not as an essence but as a performative practice.

Languaging

Earlier in this section, the reader was presented with an overview of scholarly discussions around bilingualism and the limitations of the term itself. Using the same prefix, bi, but taking the discussion towards a more fluid view of languages, straying further away from bounded entities, is the concept of bilanguaging. To understand this concept, we need to look closely at the idea of languaging. Swain proposed the concept based on Lev Vygotsky's contribution, which determines that language plays a vital role in mediating cognitive processes. According to Swain, languaging is then 'a process of making meaning and shaping knowledge and experience through language' (Swain, 2006:98). This procedural outlook embedded in the very definition of languaging sets it apart from strict linguist definitions that can sometimes be found in bilingualism studies. This term, together with translanguaging, is often seen in contexts of language pedagogy, from foreign language teaching, the multilingual classroom, or even in relation to countries with two official languages. Despite various definitions, the root word languaging implies language as a moving, constantly changing act or performance, rather than a static noun.

A concept coined and used in Applied Linguistics, languaging has been co-opted by decolonial studies to describe the types of active and emotive language use by postcolonial subjects. It has also been an accessory notion, in this area, as an active way through which postcolonial people can further decolonization practices.[16] For Argentinian semiotician Walter Mignolo, in his book *Local Histories/Global Designs: Coloniality, Subaltern Knowledges, and Border Thinking* (2012), the concept of languaging is central to denouncing the coloniality of power. As one of the main proponents of the decoloniality (*decolonialidad*) school of thought, Mignolo also proposed important terminology such as epistemic disobedience, decolonial thinking, and the coloniality of power, which are mirrored in the way he analyses examples of bilingual literature in Spanish-speaking Latin America. When debating Ambrosio Fornet's critique of 'cubanity', Mignolo defines the issue of bilingualism, bilanguaging, and their symmetries and asymmetries:

> First of all, Fornet assumes the monolanguaging principle and argues that bilingual writers have indeed a 'choice' between languages and the possibility to decide which one fits better their needs (1997:5). (...) He is right to stress that bilingualism is never symmetric, but he is wrong in assuming that bilanguaging has to be symmetric. The asymmetry of languages is not a question of a person knowing one better than the other, but it is a question of power within the diachronic internal structures of the modern world system and of its historical external borders (the colonial difference). (2012:231)

Since power dynamics are never symmetric, bilanguaging also does not have to be symmetric. Could we perhaps think of L2 translators as performing a similar languaging aesthetic? The act of making visible such asymmetries would

---

[16] For an introduction to a postcolonial take on multilingualism in literature, I recommend Arteaga (1994), Guillen (1993), and Ashcroft et al. (2004). Niranjana (1992) and Spivak (1988) are essential names for those wanting to understand language and translation within postcolonial studies.

dialogue with the idea of making visible the exteriority of language, the choices and demands involved in language use, and the underlying performativity of language practices. It is precisely because languaging is seen as language in use, language as a verb, that it can be connected to language performance and, in turn, to language drag. However, languaging is a term most used and applied in areas such as pedagogy and Applied Linguistics and our topic will benefit from seeing languaging as tied to other types of performative language practices.

Related to the idea of language performance are the propositions within gender studies of gender performance. In the next section, I will offer an overview and a proposition as to how multilingual versus monolingual language performance can be tied to the process of queering language and translation.

Language Drag

In the field of Applied Linguistics, but drawing from concepts of performativity in gender studies, linguistics, sociology, and philosophy, Pennycook (2004) proposes that we see language from an antifoundationalist perspective which takes the notion of individuals forging identities through linguistic performance. Pennycook's proposal that the 'language concept has served its time' works when it is understood as a proposal that 'would not mean that all conceptions of linguistic difference should be discarded, but rather that the over-determined sense of linguistic fixity, with its long ties to colonialism and linguistics, needs to be profoundly questioned' (Pennycook, 2004:2). The author's questioning of linguistic fixity is shared by many of the authors cited in this section thus far in my doctoral thesis. Performance, however, has direct ties with identity in language, as Pennycook asserts: 'This discussion of performativity, then, has opened up several significant ways for rethinking language and identity. Crucially, it provides a way of thinking about relationships between language and identity that emphasize the productive force of language in constituting identity rather than identity being a pregiven construct that is reflected in language use' (Pennycook, 2004:13). Therefore, if performativity in language opens up avenues towards questioning the supposed interiority of language identity and towards language identity as a performative, productive force, what then could these possible forms of language performativity be? Our first set of approaches analysed are those of language drag and language passing.

The overlap between queer studies and Translation Studies has been strongly defended by Brian James Baer in *Queer Theory and Translation Studies – Language, Politics, Desire* (2020). In the introduction, Baer draws several links between translation and queerness as both pertain otherness, borders, and difference. As the author puts it: 'The abjectification of both translation and queer sexuality can be traced to the regimes of absolute difference that emerged in the late eighteenth and early nineteenth centuries, producing modern nations as monolingual and heterosexual' (Baer, 2020:4). If monolingual is thus conceptually tied to the heterosexual, then the disruption of multilingualism could be placed with queerness as defiance to these norms.

One of the most well-known concepts within the LGBTQ+-related discourse is that of drag. The term drag is often related to drag queens, and the concept has entered the terminology of gender and sexuality studies together with queer/queerness. Once an artistic performance from the underground gay culture in New York City, the concept of drag has spread and resulted in several television shows around 'drag races', the most famous of which is RuPaul's series in the US, UK, Australia, and Canada. There is, however, a latent tense relationship between normative, heterosexually biased societies, and the disruption caused by drag performance.[17] On the disruptive aspect of drag, Fenton Litwiller explains:

> Within the performance, gender categories of the everyday are challenged by artists who intentionally sculpt a gender and production that creates gender difference. To further explain, the drag artist, by producing a gender expression (e.g., dress, mannerisms) that does not match what is expected, contests the notion that several axes of gender, including sex assigned at birth, gender expression, gender identity, and sexuality are congruent (e.g., at once assigned female at birth, with feminine expression, identify as a woman and heterosexual). (Litwiller, 2020:601)

In this explanation by Litwiller, we can see how powerful drag can be to contest notions of naturalness and congruency of gender, sex, and sexuality. Here we start seeing the possible ties between disrupting gender binaries and the assumption of congruence in gender and sex and the disruptive nature of challenging language binaries and monolingual biases in translation. Similarly, the translator who goes against monolingual norms, native-speakerism, and gatekeeping is also, in a way, disrupting the expectations involved in the many binary constructs of Translation Studies (e.g. Foreign–domestic, L1-L2, domestication–foreignization, *telos–skopos*, original–translation, source–target, sense-for-sense versus word-for-word, among several others).

---

[17] In the case of Brazil, one of the deadliest countries for LGBTQ+ while paradoxically having major record-breaking drag queen artists such as Pablo Vittar and Gloria Groove. See Atlas of Violence 2019, and Transgender Europe (TGEU) for claimed figures. See also Mendes & Da Silva (2020).

Judith Butler, the scholar who spearheaded queer and gender studies, has defined gender as performative, as something that one 'does' rather than 'is' (1990). Butler, in presenting the question of performativity, creates new possibilities and suggests that 'by interrogating implicit norms within enunciations of "identity" and recognizing it as a process of identification, something that is *done over and over* instead of something that is an *inherent* characteristic, performativity opens up new terrains of analysis' (Nelson, 1999:339). But the main theme within performativity in drag is how it ruptures and disrupts frameworks. In fact, as Litwiller puts it: 'Many renditions of drag (e.g., white drag Kings) rupture and differentiate the axis of gender because the imitative gender performance is theatrical, slightly imperfect, and campy (or so extreme as to be amusing) in ways that intentionally mock the gender framework' (Moore, 2013) (Litwiller, 2020:601). Butler (2011) puts forward the ties between drag and gender performance as '[d]rag is subversive to the extent that it reflects on the imitative structure by which hegemonic gender is itself produced and disputes heterosexuality's claim on naturalness and originality' (2011:125). Butler's definition is perhaps how we can strengthen the ties between drag's gender performativity and language drag's language performativity. Language drag comes from the idea of ethnic drag, which, according to Sieg (2002), offers some potential for us to think of language drag through the performative and disturbance lenses: 'As a technique of estrangement, drag denounces that which dominant ideology presents as natural, normal, and inescapable, without always offering another truth. As a ritual of inversion, it purports to master grave social contradictions, yet defers resolution through compulsive repetitions' (Sieg 2002:3). Therefore, language drag could be seen as a facet of ethnic drag in that it denounces dominant ideologies about language, and inverts lingualist expectations. Language drag does disrupt monolingual frameworks and translation binaries through the use of language, and these language users who do language drag do not need to have an essentialist relationship to the language, because it is an external factor, it is performative, and thus disrupts language norms. David Gramling, in the book *The Invention of Monolingualism* (2018), presents us with the conceptualization of monolingual drag as a 'form of critical doubling, monolingual drag, or an otherwise performative divestiture from the unmarked doxa of literary monolingualism' (2018:152). Connecting Gramling's to Butler's definition, then, we can think of language drag, paraphrasing Butler, as disputing monolingual claims on naturalness and originality. Drag culture involves many different types of gender performance, and the actual gender or sexuality of the drag performer is separate from their gender performance. Drag, then, is an added performative layer to that which is already performative, gender (considering Butler's proposition that gender is a social construct continually created and recreated through performative acts). If the researcher is allowed to make a connection here, one could consider that, if language is performative (Pennycook, 2004), linguistic drag is an added performative layer to that which is already performative in itself. Would translation be yet another added layer?

Gramling proposes that there also exists a 'multilingual drag', although he sees this in a more negative light, seeing it as a somewhat 'well-behaved' fake multilingual practice. Using Noorani's conceptualization of soft monolingualism (or translational monolingualism, the term Gramling uses) as 'more accessible than ever ... in that it remains within the confines of familiar linguistic norms' (Noorani, 2013:8), Gramling uses novelist Tim Park's disillusion and impatience 'with anything but wall-to-wall pre-translatedness and aesthetic exogamy' (Gramling, 2018:148) to conceptualize what he would call multilingual drag.[18] However, not all that could be perceived as language drag could be in actuality conceived as such. Some language performance could be called, simply, 'passing'.

The concept of passing is often a complex one as it can be used in the context of gender studies but also on issues of race. A person who is straight-passing has privileges in that they are not so easily identified as an LGBTQ+, and someone who is white-passing retains similar privileges in that they are not so easily the victims of racism and police brutality. Similarly, with language, some non-native speakers might enact a type of monolingual passing when they are fluent enough as to be mistaken for a native speaker, as Alison Phipps puts it:

> I have moved to 'Occupy multilingualism'. This has meant unmooring my own languages. I love to speak French and German. I worked hard to learn the languages in which I am fluent and have earned a living as a professional teacher of these in universities, I worked hard to be able to more or less 'pass', when I speak them. (Phipps, 2013:101)

Those who enact this type of passing are often criticized for enjoying privileges not offered to those who cannot pass, in any shape or form. In the case of

---

[18] To that we can add Ellen Jones's theorization on palimpsestuous writing and multilingualism in translation, present in her recent monograph *Literature in Motion: Translating Multilingualisms Across the Americas* (2022). In this book, Jones goes against the idea that multilingual texts are untranslatable. In fact, the author instead proposes that 'translation is always to some extent implied in multilingual writing' (2022:2). By going against the grain and opposing fast reading practices, Jones argues that multilingual texts and their translations call for a different reading experience, a slower, more difficult one. Jones's monograph contains good examples of how a study of a literary exophonic translation could be conducted.

language, having a stronger accent is an impediment for this type of passing, as well as having a particularly foreign-sounding name, including other characteristics.

Exophonic translator Anton Hur in an essay for the online *Litro Magazine* (2018) offers a manual on how to write queer Korean literature that has valuable ties to the work of exophonic translation. In this manual, Hur claims that most Korean literature, specifically in its thematising of suffering and tragedy, could be framed as queer literature. But most important for our purposes here is when Hur proposes that to write queer Korean literature one must 'write in translationese'. Bringing up again the concept of linguistic drag, Hur proposes that writers who 'perform' their style with translationese are 'doing language-drag. They're subtly signaling their queerness through translationese'. Claiming that disguise and performance in the language of heteronormative Korean society is a matter of survival, Hur suggests that inviting otherness in is a signal of queerness in literature. That is, escaping from a metaphorical (linguistic) closet and thus performing this otherness is an essential part of queering Korean literature and, it could be said, literature in general. The ties with exophonic performance are clear here. As we will see in Section 3, translators also act in self-fashioning their status, identity, and position in the milieus where they act, and perform a type of language drag in the process.

Exophony and Language as Prosthetics

The idea of performance, especially when contrasted with competence, is thematically tied to something external, an addition, outside of the self. Performance is how competence actually is realized in the world – a distinction similar to theory versus practice. The term exophony, with the prefix 'exo', presupposes a similar outwardness. Because of this, I will explore the concept of exophony at this textual crossroads.

Exophony: An Outward Motion

Exophony, from the Greek ἔξω, éxō, 'out, external' and φωνή, fōnē, 'sound, voice', is a term that has been recently used to refer to authors who write literature in a language other than their mother tongue (see Wright, 2008, 2010, 2013; Tawada, 2003). The term is, in a way, at the same time broad and specific. Exophony *stricto sensu* would be defined as adopting an L2 to write literature in. Exophony *lato sensu* is taken by some, like Tawada (2003), to mean that writing literature is, in itself, writing in a foreign language, so any literary text could be exophonic from this perspective. The study of exophony can then range within this spectrum, between a strict and a lax definition. By being a wide-ranging term, it can include various contexts. Exophony is a phenomenon that is increasingly fashionable nowadays, due to the new migration waves of the twenty-first century and globalisation, contributing to a context in which multilingualism and multiculturalism are more valued, at least upon a first look. This reality favours the so-called transnational literature, a more general term that includes the study of exophony.

Notions of exophony and extraterritoriality are important for the study of Comparative Literature in a twenty-first-century context, where geographical and linguistic boundaries are more fluid, and the traditional notions of art and literature seem to be going through a process of deconstruction, in which different media, voices, languages, and tongues are (or should be) in a constant dialogue. A recent term, exophony is still not part of a strong terminological tradition in many countries. The term exophony deserves a more profound analysis and a well-rounded defence of its use as a substitute for other terms and paradigms used to define cases such as Yoko Tawada's, for example. Wright (2008) offers a rich argumentation for the adoption of the term, contrasting it to other ways in which these authors and their works have been defined and studied, in this grey zone between different languages and cultures. In the article, Wright presents a few terms that could be used to describe exophonic writing but which fall short for not being inclusive enough, or not doing justice to formal features of exophonic writing. She concludes with a defence of the term exophony and the adjective exophone/exophonic as a new approach that focuses on the text. According to Wright, 'in focusing on style and how meaning is generated by it, the term "exophonic" represents an important shift in how we approach writing by non-native speakers and a return to the of late somewhat neglected relationship between form and meaning in literature' (Wright, 2008:39–40). Exophony adds certain assumptions and sociocultural contextual information that influence the reading and the translation of a text, making it a complex multi-layered literary phenomenon. Not only that, but exophonic literature

> Foregrounds how all literary texts function. ... is striking for its lack of complacency towards language, for its ability to be self-conscious and innovative in its style, not so much by drawing on the resources of another language, ... but by ceaselessly interrogating the possibilities of the adopted language and the conventions of the adopted culture. This interrogation is prompted by an awareness of the fact of linguistic and cultural difference. (Wright, 2016:138)

The concept of exophony is especially important to authors who do not fit into the traditional literary categories which are heavily dictated by the author's mother tongue or nationality. These national identities are also regularly contested, making any attachment to the national in national literature fraught and any attempt at placing exophony within these national systems a failed enterprise. Considering exophony from a stylistic point of view which focus on questions of language choice and language performance is a valid concept, even at times in which national identities were not yet fully formed or in existence.[19]

The term 'exophony', however, exists and has emerged in a world where strong national identities linked with a national language have been created and sedimented, a context in which exophonic subjects try to break free from these shackles. Exophony similarly destabilizes language and makes visible a central feature of literature, that '[a]ll literary texts, and some non-literary texts, exist in a relationship of tension between a language which belongs to everybody and a language that is the writer's own' (Wright, 2010:25). In an exophonic text this tension is heightened because the language that is the writer's own is in a different relationship to them, it is an L2. In the case of translation, and L2 translation, we add more layers of tension, making this text even more complex. Exophony is centred on the fact of creativity over fluency. It rejects that the notion of fluency is only accessible to native speakers. But beyond that, in exophony the creative possibilities trump a possible definition of fluency. Exophonic writing considers a literary language adopted by the author consciously, a move that is made external to expectations of naturalness, of linguistic nativity.

Yoko Tawada, in her travelogue-manifesto called *Ekusophonii: bogo no soto e deru tabi* (2003) (exophony: a journey outside of the mother tongue), defends some of the ideas already mentioned here throughout Sections 1 and 2 when she considers the realities of multilinguality as basis for exophonic writing:

> To write literature is at the opposite end from repeating and recombining arbitrarily the words that you hear on a daily basis. It is an attempt to face and confront the possibility of the language in which you write. By consciously doing so, the traces of your memory are highly activated and your mother tongue, your older linguistic stratum, intervenes to transform the actual language you use for Creation. When I write and read aloud sentences in German by searching the correct rhythm, my sentences come out differently from the usual, natural-sounding German. People say my sentences in German are very clear and easy to hear, but still they are 'not ordinary' and deviant in some ways. No

---

[19] Maybe one of the oldest examples of what we, in a postmonolingual paradigm, would call exophony is the case of the True Story (Ἀληθῆ διηγήματα) by Lucian of Samosata, from the II A. D., and written in Archaic Greek. The work, considered by many to be the first known work of Science Fiction, is a satire of travel writing, and extrapolates the local, by exploring extraterrestrial places. Its author, native to the Roman province of Samosata, in today's Syria, is an enigma when it comes to his mother tongue and life story, like many authors in ancient times. Lucian lived in a Roman province, wrote literature in Greek, and makes several references to his Assyrian, 'barbaric' status, and there are allusions to his origins which give way to a theory that his mother tongue would be Aramaic (Swain, 1996: 299).

wonder, because they are the results of the sound that I as an individual body have absorbed and accumulated by living through this multilingual world. It is of no use if I tried to delete my accents or remove my habits in utterance. Today a human subject is a place where different languages coexist by mutually transforming each other and it is meaningless to cancel their cohabitation and suppress the resulting distortion. Rather, to pursue one's accents and what they bring about may begin to matter for one's literary creation. (Tawada, 2003:90)[20]

Here, we can see that Tawada does make some connections to language and individual essence that may go against some of my arguments in these sections. However, it is through acceptance of this multilingual reality, of owning the accents and the interference of the mother tongue, as she calls it, that we can see the possible disruptions offered by exophonic writing. It is, in a way, performative as well, in that it shows how ordinariness and naturalness are fraught when used as yardsticks to define language ability, especially in the realm of translation.

For the longest time Translation Studies could get away with studying the history and the theory of translation based on these monological concepts we discussed in the previous sections. As we have seen from Section 1, the L1 norm in Translation Studies also caused L2 translation and its practitioners to remain invisible, chastised for attempting to go against the grain. When any area of study turns to human beings as subjects, it becomes necessary to consider the idiosyncrasies of working with the varied and unique experiences of each individual. In the section that follows, I will present an overview of an incipient area of Translation Studies dedicated to the study of the agents involved in translation, called sociology of translation, or TranslaTOR Studies. This sociological turn in Translation Studies considers the agents and external factors that influence the way translations are received in different cultures, as well as the role of the translator within different cultural polysystems. Studies that focus on the translator cannot be bound by outdated, prescriptive norms and based on idealized subjects. These studies must deal with the real translators behind a translation act, and with these some of the

---

[20] 文学を書くということは、いつも耳から入ってきている言葉をなんとなく繋ぎ合わせて繰り返すこ との逆で、言語の可能性とぎりぎりまで向かい合うということだ。そうすると、記憶の痕跡がたくさん活性化され、古い層である母語が今使っている言語をデフォルメするのかもしれない。だから自分がこれだと思うドイツ語のリズムを探して文章を作り、それを朗読する時には、いわゆ る自然そうな日常ドイツ語からは離れる。ドイツ語として聞いていて大変聞き取りやすいとはよく 言われるが、それでもどこか「普通」ではない。それはまず何より、わたしという個体がこの多言 語世界で吸収してきた音の集積である。ここでなまりや癖をなくそうとすることには意味がない。むしろ、現代では、一人の人間というのは、複数の言語がお互いに変形を強いながら共存している 場所であり、その共存と歪みそのものを無くそうとすることには意味がない。むしろ、なまりその ものの結果を追求していくことが文学創造にとって意味を持ちはじめるかもしれない。

monotopical, restrictive language norms behind translation theory will hopefully fail to hold their ground.

3 Translators under the Microscope

Another essential aspect of humanized Translation Studies is the role of the individual. As the overview of past developments has shown, translators have long been excluded from theoretical models of translation, regarded as machine-like translator-ideals or as a homogeneous collective. In an effort to find common denominators and universally valid general principles, the translatorial individual was lost. (...). In contrast, the humanizing approach does not see translators as abstract units, but as 'people with flesh-and-blood bodies' (Pym, 1998:161). Consequently, they are perceived as individuals against a social and cultural background, who are subject to contextual and situational constraints, and thus become visible as real people. (Kaindl, 2021:11)

And Who Translates the Translator?

James Holmes's seminal essay 'The Name and Nature of Translation Studies' (1972/1988) is often regarded as the foundation of Translation Studies. Holmes advocated for a translation sociology, emphasizing the importance of understanding the agents behind the translation process rather than solely focusing on the translation product. Andrew Chesterman furthered this discourse by advocating more strongly for sociological studies in translation, proposing 'The Name and Nature of Translator Studies' (2009), referencing Holmes's work. Chesterman critiques the predominant focus on the function of translation, derived from *Skopos* Theory, while neglecting the translator's approach, termed *telos* in the same theory. Translation Studies historically overlooked the cognitive, social, and cultural constraints on translators' work until the cultural turn in the 1990s brought attention to these issues. Descriptive translation studies revealed power structures but failed to acknowledge translators as active agents (Prunč, 2007). Translation process research integrated cognitive aspects but lacked consideration of social determinants until the late 1990s' sociological turn, spearheaded by Theo Hermans. Scholars like Michaela Wolf and others applied sociological concepts, particularly Bourdieu's *habitus*, to analyse translation and translators, leading to the emergence of translation sociology (or TranslaTOR Studies).[21] Wolf (2007) delineates three sociologies: of agents, process, and cultural product. According to Schögler (2017), translation as a social practice encompasses micro-, meso-, and macro-structural factors,

---

[21] Key names in Translation Sociology include Michaela Wolf, Héléne Buzelin, Andrew Chesterman, Klaus Kaindl, Luise von Flotow (especially for Feminist Translation Studies), Jean-Marc Gouanvic, Giséle Sapiro, Theo Hermans, and Daniel Simeoni, among many others.

elucidating the dynamics between translators, institutions, and broader societal developments. Klaus Kaindl's (2021) collection on Literary Translator Studies underscores the need for specific research on literary translators' practices, reflecting an interdisciplinary approach within Translation Studies. Despite its heterogeneity, translation sociology underscores the interconnectedness of agents, processes, and products in translation, offering a rich framework for studying L2 translation and exophony.

Heilbron (1999) introduces the concept of a world system of translation (referencing Wallerstein's world system theory). By viewing translations as 'a function of the social relations between language groups and their transformations over time' (1999:430), Heilbron emphasizes the importance of understanding translation dynamics within a larger systemic context. He suggests that translations offer indirect access to an emerging world language system, highlighting the complex interplay between linguistic communities and multilingual speakers. Therefore, using polysystemic lens, translation is seen as transnational cultural exchange, revealing power structures and core periphery tensions within the global flow of translated books. Heilbron's analysis underscores the significance of comprehending the various subsystems and levels of agency in the translation process to grasp the complexity of the international translation system and its impact on cultural dynamics.

The varying role of translation in different language groups further elucidates the intricate relationship between translation and social dynamics. Heilbron's sociological perspective emphasizes the socio-historical context and power dynamics shaping translation practices. The centrality of certain languages in the international translation system, particularly English, influences the distribution and diversity of translated works. Heilbron's analysis also sheds light on the role of cultural institutions and economic factors in facilitating translation flows and shaping literary markets. However, discrepancies in translation statistics highlight the complex interplay between centrality in the world-book system and the proportion of translations in national book production, suggesting that cultural importation is contingent upon a language group's global significance rather than solely its cultural richness.

For L2 translation this complex literary translation eco- and polysystem has important implications. When minority, endangered, indigenous, or otherwise less-widely diffused languages are translated into a hyper-central language such as English, the risks of cultural appropriation, exoticization, and erasure, among others, are high and must be debated. In World Literature there is already an ongoing debate about this topic, and translators of colour have spoken publicly about these risks as well. It is important to make clear that L2 translation presents itself (both in theory and in practice) through translators of less-widely diffused languages, known by fewer (or no) native English users capable of translating from them to a high standard. In these contexts, historical relay, or indirect translation, has been used, but maybe more interestingly, collaborative translation has turned out, in some cases, to be an answer to these 'problems'.[22] Pokorn (2005) presents a more in-depth analysis and defence of collaborative translation regarding L2 translation practices. Perhaps in future research a specific question about collaboration in L2 translation would be beneficial to understanding this practice better and framing it in a way that dialogues with exophonic translation.

The Translator's *Habitus*

In Chesterman's (2007) exploration of translation sociology, he contends that translation research offers quasi-causes, not grounded in lawlike regularity, due to the translator's cognitive mediation. This emphasis on human agency places translation sociology at the forefront, focusing on the translator's practice, discourse, and habitus. Borrowing from Bourdieu (1977), habitus in translation sociology refers to the amalgamation of external and structural factors with the translator's agency, serving as a lens through which societal influence shapes individual dispositions and responses. Bourdieu's conceptualization of habitus transcends the dichotomy between structure and agency, illustrating how societal structures inform an individual's disposition and capacity to navigate social demands. Furthermore, habitus operates as a dynamic system of dispositions that evolves over time and context, influenced by external forces such as migration and specialized training (Wacquant, 2018:3). By understanding habitus, researchers gain insight into how social conditions shape individuals' beliefs, behaviours, and practices in translation, highlighting the complexity of social dynamics within the translator's domain.

In the context of literary translation, the translator's habitus plays a pivotal role in shaping both translation decisions and the positioning of translated works within different cultural systems. Scholars like Wolf (1999, 2002, 2003) and Matter-Seibel (2006) have applied Bourdieu's framework to analyse various aspects of literary translation, including ideological contexts, feminist translation, and the impact of gender on translation practices. For instance, Matter-Seibel's (2006) study on Margaret Fuller's translations of German

---

[22] The use of problems between quote marks here is because, even though I do not believe L2 translation is necessarily a problem, many in the industry and within translation studies would not agree with me or with the L2 translation scholars mentioned in Section 1.

literature into English demonstrates how the translator's habitus can import new ideas and influence societal discourse. Similarly, Schweiger's (2006) investigation into the relationship between author and translator reveals how the translator's habitus can affect the reception and positioning of foreign authors within different literary systems. These studies underscore the significance of the translator's habitus in shaping not only translation practices but also the cultural and social impact of translated works within diverse linguistic and literary contexts. Applying such a view of *habitus* to this work, for example, we could say that the L1 translation norm entered these social strata of translation theory and practice resulting in dispositions through which the practice of translating into a second language became discouraged. L1 translators who are also monolingual anglophones have been discouraged from trying this direction of translation and thus also assume that such must be the reality of all translators. To put it simply, if I cannot do it, no one can. However, L2 translators seem to fight against such restrictive, normative views. The *habitus* of translators, in general, as we have seen, can be changed when exposed to external forces. What would be the external forces necessary to change such a strong *habitus*-informing rule like the L1 translation norm?

The Translator: Real or Ideal?

The two historically known *habiti* of the translator are, as defined by Erich Prunč (2007), Priests and Pariahs. The author points out two diametrically opposed and somewhat schizophrenic expectations placed upon translators and translations, both within Translation Studies and in wider society. Translators are both at the centre and at the margins of our transcultural exchanges. Prunč proposed that, historically, translators position themselves somewhere on this spectrum where the poles are either subservient or carriers of the truth. According to his definition,

> [t]he translator-priests see themselves as the guardians of the word and as the gate keepers and constructors of culture. They know that they have the power to select, to transform and to define, which also provides them with the key to socially accepted values and truths. The *habitus* of the translator-priest first emerged in Mesopotamia. (...) It was later adopted by the great bible translators St. Jerome and Luther and also by literary translators whose creations have become an integral part of national literary canons. (Prunč, 2007:48–49)

Therefore, translators can act as gatekeepers as well, choosing who can enter their realm and be accepted as their peers, as well as defining the limits and quality of literary culture and practice. This translator-priest holds power in their literacy. In literary translation, this is a translator who can become a mentor for emerging translators, win awards, and get competitive grants. In publishing, sometimes a successful literary translator may become the head of a publishing house or an acquisitions editor, for example.[23] Translators who enjoy prestige, be it because of their connections, the language they translate from/into or other factors, often hold what translation sociologists call a 'symbolic capital' over others in the profession. As Prunč puts it:

> Translators may also gain significant symbolic capital if they choose prestigious languages as their working languages – even if this may run counter to the requirements of the market and the dominance of supply and demand. A good example is the demand for the less widely spoken and less widely taught languages and the prestige of translators, working in these languages. (Prunč, 2007:45)

Therefore, this prestige that Prunč speaks of may also come from some translators' access to highly coveted language combinations and is also dependent on some contextual determinators. For example, prestigious awards like the International Booker Prize can result in renewed interest in a language, author, or literature (e.g. translator Daisy Rockwell and author Geetanjali Shree for the Hindi novel *Tomb of Sand* (2021), International Booker Prize and Nobel Prize winner Olga Tokarczuk (in translation by Jennifer Croft) in 2018–19). Similar external factors that may affect prestige and demand for certain language combinations include the status of the translator; for example, Ann Goldstein's decades-long work for the prestigious *New Yorker* magazine and her translations of Elena Ferrante's Neapolitan Quartet which contributed to the recent Ferrante Fever.[24] Another example presented by researcher Motoko Akashi (2018, 2021; Hadley & Akashi, 2015) is that of Haruki Murakami's work as a translator of US literature into Japanese and his celebrity status in Japan. His celebrity status is so substantial that a book series with his translations was created in Japan, titled Haruki Murakami Translated Library, with his name mentioned on the cover in order to boost sales.

Prunč also defines the other end of the spectrum – that of the translator-pariah – as follows:

> The *habitus* of the pariah is the most extreme version of the *habitus* of the 'quintessential servant', as Simeoni (1998:12) puts it. This *habitus* is the relic of the historic marginalisation of translators and the result of their other or self-imposed invisibility. Translators who adopt this *habitus* consider the

---

[23] This is the case of, for example, International Booker prize winner Deborah Smith who started Tilted Axis Press, although she has stepped down and made Kristen Alfaro sole publishing director.

[24] For more on this, see the documentary Ferrante Fever (2017).

author and poet as their master, the customer as the king. They continue to work for ever lower prices and rates and are both the victims and originators of the current price-cutting spiral (cf. Prunč, 2003) which threatens not only their own existence but also the reputation of the translation profession. (Prunč, 2007:49)

In this respect, there is, however, a deep precipice between literary and technical (or often called 'professional') translators, especially in their self-fashioning. Some studies in translation sociology deal with literary translators constructing an image of themselves as very distinct in their practice when compared to translators of non-literary texts. Sela-Sheffy (2016), for example, looked at Israeli cases, but some of her conclusions could be expanded to other contexts:

> I argue that at least in the Israeli case, which may be analogous to other cultural settings, the status structure in the field of translation and interpreting is shaped by a prevailing counter-professionalisation ethos, and that this ethos is nurtured by a restricted circle of elite literary translators. This means that the occupational identity and sense of personal agency cultivated by this small sector is what prevents the construction of institutional tools and determines the hierarchy in the field at large. This further means that despite the loose structure of the field and its division into different branches, it is governed by a more or less 'unified symbolic market', to use Bourdieu's terminology (1995), in which literary translators are those who set the symbolic prices. (Sela-Sheffy, 2016:57)

This counter-professionalisation ethos that Sela-Sheffy speaks of works well with the image of literary translators as artists but does not do much for their professionalization. The very fact that Translation Studies creates the same division between literary translation and 'everything else' does not help us see that, if we look closely, there is an underlying translationality to all translations, no matter if they are technical or artistic. On this gap between literary and non-literary translators, Sela-Sheffy relates:

> The two archetypes that fuel the counter-professionalisation dynamics in the field of translatorial occupations, the artist and the natural translator, are promoted by the two sectors most remote from each other and from the mainstream of active translators and interpreters – high-status literary translators, on the one hand, and lower-ranked community interpreters, on the other. Yet unlike the latter, top literary translators have a sound vision of their role and privileges. Therefore, their authority as the producers and regulators of the symbolic capital of this occupation is not challenged. This also means, however, that the artisation ethos – what in the eyes of top literary translators distinguishes them from the majority of non-elite stranslators – actually permeates the field at large beyond their own circle. (Sela-Sheffy, 2016:68)

Here, Sela-Sheffy creates a further two archetypes: the artist and the natural translator, putting community interpreters and high-status literary translators at opposite ends of the spectrum. In between, we may have anything ranging from literary translators who are published by smaller presses or have publications in not-for-profit journals to audiovisual translators, localisation professionals, and court interpreters. In the pool of translators interviewed for my thesis, at least half of them are literary translators whose main source of income is, according to them, non-literary translation. These subjects, then, are found somewhere in between this spectrum, aspiring to a translatorial occupation that encompasses the artistic but who, for financial sustainability, need to do the 'dirty work' of non-literary translation.

It follows that Prunč and Sela-Sheffy's categorizations are not equivalent. There are those in the literary translation world who act as the 'quintessential servant' and claim translation is merely a labour of love, as much as there are others who see themselves as the artist-translator. Sometimes, whether consciously or unconsciously, literary translators may position themselves as superior to their non-literary colleagues, or, to use Prunč's terms, position themselves as the priests/artists to the other's pariah.

Levels of Consecration

On the degrees of consecration and the work of exophonic translators, Lindqvist (2006) offers, in her analysis of the Swedish field of literary translation, a model which will be useful and taken into consideration in this Element. Positioned agents in the field of literary translation have control over the symbolic capital, in this case the cultural capital of translation, and assign value to other agents. Therefore, the agents' position and status in the field is determined by their level of access to cultural capital. According to Lindqvist, 'an interesting step towards a description of translation as a social practice is to map out the consecration mechanisms of the posited fields under study' (2006:67). Consecration, taken from the Catholic tradition, means to bestow upon someone a merit, usually to be made or considered sacred. A specific field can have a structure of consecration mechanisms for the agent in that field to reach the highest point of consecration.

In the case of literary translators in the UK, for example, we have the Officer of the Most Excellent Order of the British Empire recently awarded to translator Daniel Hahn. Being accepted as a fellow of the Royal Academy or British Academy can also work as consecration mechanisms. These peaks in the consecration scale are context-specific, as Lindqvist points out that in the Swedish context of high-prestige literary translation these would translate to an appointment as honorary professor of translation by the government. However, these are also bound by source-language prestige in the specific context. In the UK, for example, most of the high-prestige literary translators translate from European languages such as French, German, Spanish, Portuguese, Russian, and Scandinavian. If it is true that in order to describe and analyse translation as a social practice these mechanisms need to be mapped out, then in order to have a sociology of translation it is necessary to carry out analyses of the fields in which translation circulates and of the agents involved in the process.

In this sense, investigating the positioning of exophonic translators in these power dynamics and different systems can be fruitful for understanding who these participants in the translation world are. Here, it is worth expanding on Lindqvist to highlight the consecration mechanisms in the specific case of exophonic translators. Inspired by Bourdieu's autonomous fields, Lindqvist constructs a general model for reconstruction of consecration mechanisms, which she separates into four phases, in order from a lower degree to a higher degree of consecration: the investment phase, the initiation phase, the recognition phase, and the confirmation phase. To be considered a translator, a newcomer needs to invest in education, visibility, improvement, networking, and alliances with positioned agents, be those colleagues, publishers, professors, and in general opinion-makers. In many cases this comes in the form of professionalisation courses – at universities or specific translation institutes – and in the form of workshops. Of course, translators usually come to the profession via different routes, but this is one of the most traditional. The initiation phase usually consists of similar steps as the investment stage – it means for most contexts entry-level jobs, some freelancing and pitching books for publishers and journals. When a translator has a published work, they can be considered to have entered the recognition phase. With a few published works, the translator, according to Lindqvist, then becomes a positioned agent in their field, able to influence, at least to a small degree, others. After moving beyond the recognition phase, and

> [e]ntering [the recognition stage] of consecration, the translator becomes subject to appreciative awards for his/her work in the form of scholarships, prizes or prestigious appointments. He/she will at this stage be asked to write prologues or epilogues in connection with his/her work in order to explain his/her translational practice. The translator's practice is thus deemed worthwhile. The moment the translator is asked to join the board of one of the institutions responsible for the scholarships, prizes, or prestigious appointments, he/she has reached one of the possible peaks of the consecration scale. (Lindqvist, 2006:69)

This discussion on consecration takes us back to high-status literary translators and their symbolic capital. It is not difficult to see how those who possess such capital do not necessarily want to part with it and will inevitably decide on those who can and cannot make the same art largely through norms based on their own subjectivity. This means that some consecrated, high-status translators who do not feel comfortable translating into an L2 might unconsciously assume this is true for the whole profession, and result in gatekeeping literary translation basing it on the trite L1-direction dictum.

Norms and Dispositions

Since *habitus* is a term that deals closely with dispositions of social groups, often professional, as is the case of translator habiti, then a discussion about norms, albeit brief, needs to take place at this stage. Gideon Toury and Theo Hermans (1999, 2007) are the two main contributors to the idea of norms in translation. In Toury's theory, translation is a norm-governed activity which considers two sets of norm systems: that of the source and of the target language – what he calls 'initial norms' (Toury, 1995:56). Toury splits these norms into preliminary norms (viz. translation policy and directness of translation) and operational norms (viz. matricial norms and textual-linguistic norms). Since Toury's proposal, these norms are seen as product norms and process norms. Andrew Chesterman (1997) takes Toury's translation norms and proposes his own: expectancy norms (equivalent to product norms) and professional norms (equivalent to process). According to him, expectancy norms are those which are largely dependent on the target language and culture of a translation and could determine whether a translation is considered acceptable or not. He concludes by saying that '[e]xpectancy norms, then, are not static or permanent, nor are they monolithic. They are highly sensitive to text-type – not all text-types are necessarily expected to conform consistently to fluent standard usage – and they are open to modification and change' (Chesterman, 1997:67). The other type of norm, the professional norms, according to him, are those often voiced by certain actors in the translation process. As he puts it, 'the norm authorities par excellence are perhaps those members of the society who are deemed to be competent professional translators, whom the society trusts as having this status, and who may further be recognized as competent professionals by other societies also' (Chesterman, 1997:67). These norm authorities will then set the standards which others in the profession will follow. Such standards include textual and linguistic strategies, for example.

Following this categorization, the L1 translation norm would find itself within the preliminary norms that Toury speaks of and both of Chesterman's proposed expectancy and professional norms. A study on literary exophonic translation would therefore concern itself with how these translators deal with norms against their practice, which are external to the micro-decisions of the actual texts involved, concerning itself then with the behaviour, normative or not, of L2, or exophonic translators. To conclude, Toury asserts:

> [N]on-normative behaviour is always a possibility. The price for selecting this option may be as low . . .. However, it may also be far more severe . . .; which is precisely why non-normative behaviour tends to be the exception, in actual practice. On the other hand, in retrospect, deviant instances of behaviour may be found to have effected changes in the very system. . . . Implied are intriguing questions such as who is 'allowed' by a culture to introduce changes and under what circumstances such changes may be expected to occur and/or be accepted. (Toury, 1995:64)

Therefore, the existence of norms is necessary to regulate a system such as that of translation, but we must never ignore the fact that there is non-normative behaviour. In the case of L2 translation and the question of directionality, one must ask perhaps if this non-normative, disruptive behaviour of translating against the grain would not have the potential to change the very norms they are fighting against. However, again, coming back to Toury's citation, not all are 'allowed' to introduce such changes.

An Exophonic Translation Sociology?

Therefore, translation sociology helps us shed light on the subject doing the translation, and the context in which it happens. Since the aim of my study is to see how exophonic translation can be innovative because it focuses on creative aspects, attitudes, and relationship to the text and languages/cultures involved, the field of translation sociology plays an important part. Toury accounts for the fact that normative formulations 'imply other interests, particularly a desire to control behaviour – i.e. to dictate norms rather than merely account for them' (1995:55). This occurs partly when descriptive turns into prescriptive. Scholars are yet undecided on when exactly the L1 translation norm turned from descriptive to prescriptive, perhaps it was born the latter. However, as Toury puts it: 'Normative formulations tend to be slanted, then, and should always be taken with a grain of salt' (Toury, 1995:55). The *habitus* of the L2/exophonic translator is where we can see a major difference between these and other translators. The fact that exophonic translators are going against the directionality norm in Translation Studies and the translation market points to an overall influence on their beliefs about language and translation, with hopes that rules about translation are more descriptive, empiric, embodied, and thus more concerned with the actual agents behind this practice.

Exophonic Translators on Their Practice

Although we can find examples of studies dealing with L2 translation within academia, and we must be aware that such studies might arise from personal interest and the experience of the scholars on the topic of directionality (meaning that they themselves have done L2 translation in their practice), there is value in seeing how exophonic translators who are not necessarily speaking to an academic audience write about their practice in essays and translator commentaries. Not all literary L2 translators have written, or rather made public, their thoughts on directionality and exophony. The following examples offer a glimpse and adequately wrap up the topics raised thus far.

In a piece published in *The Linguist* magazine in 2017, translator and editor Marta Dziurosz discusses her experience and her views in 'On (L2) Non-native Translation'. She chooses to call the practice 'Bilingual Translation' and recollects her own personal history with this practice and what she has encountered regarding it in the literary translation context.[25] Recounting an episode at a literary fair when someone questioned the desire of a member of the audience to translate into their L2, Dziurosz is surgical when she concludes that '[t]his was the first of many instances I witnessed of bilingual translation being treated as whimsical at best, and gross incompetence at worst.' I have come across similar instances, and in fact cannot recall a time when 'bilingual translation' was described as something positive. Dziurosz goes on to discuss this bias inherent in the literary translation world, specifically the facet that puts native speakers on a pedestal. She then proposes that a research project aiming at uncovering editors' and publishers' implicit bias would be of great interest. Translators I have interviewed point out several instances where they fell victim to this kind of implicit monolingual bias at the hands of publishers and editors. Dziurosz, mentioning an informal survey she conducted and an event she organized on the topic, concludes that categories of native and non-native are, in fact, obsolete, or rather should be made to become obsolete. She proposes, in fact, that we should 'retire' such terminology.

In a longer piece about her practice, entitled 'Neither Here And There: The Misery and Splendor of (Reverse) Translation', Bulgarian translator Ekaterina Petrova (2020) goes into detail on her process of both coming to terms with translation in both directions and how she sees her own relationship to this practice and the practice of translating multi-directionally itself. As we can see

---

[25] When discussing the terminology around L2 translation in Section 1, I mention the term bilingual translator and present more reasons as to why I choose not to adopt it. When we see the linguistic backgrounds and realities of the exophonic translators interviewed in Collischonn (2023), it becomes clear that bilingual is inadequate to cover the multiplicity of their complex language relations.

from her title, she names this practice reverse translation. Interestingly, she places the word 'reverse' in parentheses, alluding to the possibility of it just being called 'translation'. This is something that Dziurosz broaches in her essay, when she mentions: 'A large number of my respondents did not define themselves as bilingual translators – just as translators.' Explaining her choice of word, Petrova elucidates how the practice is 'colloquially known [in Bulgarian] as *obraten prevod*, which literally means 'reverse translation'. As an adjective, *obraten* carries the negative connotation of something abnormal or backward, something that goes against the grain, or something that simply isn't right. As a noun, *obraten* is used as a derogatory slur for a queer person'.[26] In here, the very choice of terminology to describe L2 translation can bring with it a value judgement. Petrova's essay revolves around some of the assumptions that lie behind the L1 norm, which I paraphrase here as, firstly, that monolingualism is the norm; secondly, that language ownership and national identity are conflated; thirdly, that language is a discrete, monolithic entity; finally, that an individual's relationship with their language, whatever that may be, is fixed and unchanging. Petrova, in fact, sums up a great deal of what can be found in this and in following sections, and what we can see in the interviews with exophonic translators. Claiming to feel at home in both Bulgarian and English, Petrova admits to her Bulgarian being perceived as 'fluent', while her English is simply 'accented'. She then explains further her own experiences with gatekeeping:

> Even if I could erase the accent, the cold, clingy, non-negotiable facts of my name, my place of birth, and my nationality are enough to make all these intricacies, complicated relationships, and my own particular biographical details vanish into thin air. The mere, usually unavoidable, mention of these facts, either together or separately, often seems sufficient to bring into question not just the quality of my translations and the validity of my approaches or decisions, but also my legitimacy as a translator of Bulgarian into English as a whole. Even in friendly and well-meaning scenarios, I've often had to rationalize it; in less benevolent ones, I've had to actively defend it.

This issue of name and accent was brought up by some of the translators I interviewed, and I myself have come across anecdotal evidence for this. When translating into English, some translators whose names are clearly not anglophone-sounding very often face an eyebrow-raising of sorts Petrova

---

[26] The fact that *obraten* is a derogatory slur for a queer person and happens to also be, together with *prevod*, the Bulgarian term for L2 translation makes the connection between queer textual practices and exophonic writing and translation a stronger one. I aim to explore this in future work.

speaks of. In the case of Petrova, it helps that she can add to her curriculum vitae an MFA from the renowned Literary Translation programme in Iowa. She credits the programme director, Aron Aji, an exophonic translator himself (although he prefers the terminology bilingual translator) as he worked to include more translators who are not L1 translators. It seems that in some of the hubs of literary translation teaching, like the Iowa MFA programme, and in the UK context the BCLT Summer School and the National Centre for Writing Mentorship programmes, among others, there has been a slow shift towards more acceptance of the practice and having exophonic/bilingual translators at the helm seems to have helped with this shift.

But it is when reflecting on directionality and target versus source language in the process of translating that Petrova brings up an especially valid point: that every translator will inevitably have their shortcomings, be it in the understanding of the source language or in creating a text in the target language. In her own words,

> [w]hether we admit it or not, we all have blind spots – it's just that for some of us, they might be mostly in the source language, and for others, mostly in the target one. As a way to calm down, counteract my occasional sense of impostor syndrome, and avoid getting paralyzed, I tell myself that I might actually be in a more favourable position than my native-speaker peers. This is because, even when I mess up, the kinds of mistakes that I'm likely to make will almost certainly get caught and corrected by the Anglophone editors of my translations. By contrast, mistakes resulting from failing to understand something in the original are much more difficult to catch, especially when that original is in a 'small' language that is usually completely inaccessible to the English or American editors of the translation.

Here, Petrova mirrors Dziurosz's previously mentioned notion of the inherent strengths and weaknesses we can find in the process of translation, whatever the directionality. It is precisely when talking about the imperfectness of the translation act, and product, that Petrova drives home one of her main points: that by not owing loyalty to either language she is able to detach from them, to not see them as 'sacred', as she puts it. This detachment is similarly found in exophonic literary works as the ability to see a language from the point of view of a foreigner can have innovative implications for works of literature. This is discussed in detail in Section 2 and in this section. Seeing language as performative, external to the self, is, in fact, one of the interpretative nodes of this work, as we saw earlier in this Element. Petrova and Dziurosz are L2 translators who have experienced the L1 translation norm and have faced some of the weaknesses of this translation dictum. Their texts are used here to introduce some of the problematics brought forth by the L1 translation fiat. They also help us understand that there is a systemic bias against bilingual subjects in Translation Studies, and an untested and unquestioned preference for monotopic ideas of language.

Exophonic Translation or Exophonic TranslaTORs?

We know that the history of how L2 translation has been seen in Translation Studies has been invisible at best, fraught with assumptions and lack of evidence to support the L1 translation norm. We also know that in adjacent fields like applied linguistics, multilingualism studies, and postcolonial studies, the debunking of the native speaker myth has been happening for quite a while and progressed in ways that have not been taken on by Translation Studies. We know that in Literary Translation Studies the L2-L1 directionality is the default. The expanding field of Translator Studies has made it possible, making available new methods, and opened new research avenues that can be applied to exophonic translation. In this Element, my goal is to propose that, considering what we have seen in this element, literary L2 translation can be structured around the exophonic outlook, and use methods from translation sociology to further the field. At this point in time, understanding of the problems involved in a L1 norm in translated literature is still at its infancy. Thus, our answers are limited. The invisibility of L2 translations makes for a lack of knowledge around existing L2 literary translations in the market. The existing attempts at an answer are limited to understanding the people behind these translations, and their views on their practice. I can mention a few examples here of translators who we could say, with some degree of certainty, would accept the exophonic outlook, or label. These are, of course, limited to those I have encountered, in languages that I can more or less access, and in varying degrees of consecration in the literary market. We have a few representatives across different languages, such as Anton Hur, Amaia Gabantxo, Bruna Dantas Lobato, Julia Sanches, and Jeremy Tiang, among several others. Bruna, for example, is a US-based Brazilian author and translator who recently won the 2023 National Book Award for her translation of *The Words That Remain*, by Stenio Gardel and published *Blue Light Hours* (2024), her first novel in English. Sanches is a prolific translator of Portuguese, Spanish, and Catalan into English, with many awards and nominations to her name; Amaia Gabantxo is a Basque translator and musician who often takes on challenging translation projects and champions her minority language in translation. Anton Hur is prolific award-winning translator and author who has been shortlisted for the International Booker Prize more than once and sits on prestigious awards' judging panels. Other examples include Kotryna Garanasvilli, Antonella Lettieri, Kairani Barokka, Cecilia Rossi, Nariman Youssef, Emily Yae Won, Marta Dziurosz, Alice Olsson, and the list could truly go on and on. What unites all these translators mentioned here would perhaps be not having a straightforward answer to what is their L1 or L2, or challenging the L1 translation norm and proving that the practice of exophonic translation is not only a reality but can also result in creatively rich outcomes in literary translation. The study of literary exophonic translation should ideally focus on the translator and their attitudes to the text and to language as opposed to a textual analysis based on naturalness, fluency, and acceptability by the native speaker/reader. A close reading or a text-based analysis can greatly contribute to our understanding. However, one must leave their L2 prejudices behind and strive to be less native-speakerist when analysing translation outputs.

4 Coda

This is a work of epistemic disobedience (Mignolo, 2009). L2 translation and a theory in defence of this practice are also, in a way, a confrontation of Eurocentric or Anglocentric modes of thinking in Translation Studies, aiming at an epistemic reconstruction. However, we can attest that there is a miscommunication between theories, norms, and actual practice. Even with many groundbreaking studies going against the monolingual norm, the L1 translation norm, and other norms which uphold these Euro and Anglocentric epistemes around translation, there is still a great deal of disobedience needed. I propose that we invert linguist expectations about translation, that we ask for a bi-/multilingual/ exophonic turn to Translation Studies, where binaries that thus far upheld outdated norms can be found as something to oppose, as a reactive, interactive basis, but not as the end-all of translation theory.

The topics debated here create the basis for the question: Who is this language practitioner who goes against the unquestioned norms about directionality in translation? Who is the literary exophonic translator? In an interdisciplinary exploration of the topic, this Element is an attempt to shed light on non-conformist creative linguistic practices and show how pervasive and untested the rules against L2 translation are, offering an approach for future studies on literary L2 translation.

In conclusion, it seems Translation Studies, and most of the anglophone publishing market, with the L1 translation norm, are imprisoned of their own accord in what Walter D. Mignolo terms 'monotopic hermeneutics of modernity and nationalism' (1996:189),[27] with the monological bulwarks and bastions of the discipline still myopic to the realities of translation on the global scale, and blind to the breakthroughs and discussions happening in other disciplines

---

[27] 'Theorizing languages within social structures of domination is dealing with the "natural" plurilingual conditions of the human world "artificially" suppressed by the monolingual ideology and monotopic hermeneutics of modernity and nationalism' (Mignolo, 1996: 189).

regarding the native speaker, monolingualism, and multilingualism. However, metalinguistic discourse is changing, and alongside come language users breaking through culture maintenance to bring culture change.

It is in the tension between what exophonic translators were taught and what they do that the power of literary exophonic translation might lie. And making this tension visible is what we strive to convey. As exophonic poet and scholar Keijiro Suga once said:

> Exophony is not something special for literature. It is rather a basic condition of an innovative literary language that is always trying to implode and break its own vessel from within. Only through self-destruction can a language obtain a new life. [O]ur common destiny in today's translational poetics is to pursue one's own accents, to retain all the memories of linguistic collision that one has gone through. (Suga, 2007:27)

May literary exophonic translation offer a way to retain all of these linguistic collisions via translation.

References

Akashi, M. (2018). 'Translator celebrity: Investigating Haruki Murakami's visibility as a translator', *Celebrity Studies*, 9(2), pp. 271–278.

Akashi, M. (2021). 'Manifestations of creativity: Murakami Haruki as translator', in Hansen, G. M. and Tsang, M. (eds.), *Murakami Haruki and Our Years of Pilgrimage*. Oxford: Routledge, pp. 219–239.

Alderson, J. C. (1980). 'Native and nonnative speaker performance on cloze tests', *Language Learning*, 30(1), pp. 59–76.

Alighieri, D. (1896). *Il Trattato De vulgari eloquentia*. Edited by P. Rajna. Florence: Le Monnier.

Alim, H. S. (2016a). 'Introducing raciolinguistics: Racing language and languaging race in hyperracial times', in Alim, H. S., Rickford, J. R., and Ball, A. (eds.), *Raciolinguistics: How Language Shapes Our Ideas about Race*. New York: Oxford University Press, pp. 1–30.

Alim, H. S. (2016b). 'Who's afraid of the transracial subject? Raciolinguistics and the political project of transracialization', in Alim, H. S., Rickford, J. R., and Ball, A. F. (eds.), *Raciolinguistics*. Oxford: Oxford University Press, pp. 33–50.

Anderson, B. (1983). *Imagined Communities: Reflections on the Origin and Spread of Nationalism*. 25th ed. London: Verso.

Aneja, G. A. (2016). 'Rethinking nativeness: Toward a dynamic paradigm of (non) native speakering', *Critical Inquiry in Language Studies*, 13(4), pp. 351–379.

Arteaga, A. (1994a). *An Other Tongue: Nation and Ethnicity in the Linguistic Borderlands*. Durham, NC: Duke University Press.

Baer, B. J. (2020). *Queer Theory and Translation Studies: Language, Politics, Desire*. London/New York: Routledge.

Baker, C. (2001). *Foundations of Bilingual Education and Bilingualism*. 3rd ed. Tonawanda: Multilingual Matters.

Baker, M. (2000). Towards a methodology for investigating the style of a literary translator. *Target*, 12, pp. 241–266.

Baker, W. (2009). 'The cultures of English as a lingua franca on JSTOR', *TESOL Quarterly*, 43(4), pp. 567–592.

Bassetti, B. (2012). 'Bilingualism and writing systems', in Bhatia, T. K. and Ritchie, W. C. (eds.), *The Handbook of Bilingualism and Multilingualism*. Hoboken, NJ: John Wiley & Sons, pp. 649–670.

Bassnett, S., and Lefevere, A. (1990). *Translation, History and Culture*. London: Printer Publishers.

Bassnett, S., and Lefevere, A. (eds.) (1998). *Constructing Cultures: Essay on Literary Translation*. Clevedon: Multilingual Matters.

Bauman, R., and Briggs, C. L. (2003). *Voices of Modernity: Language Ideologies and the Politics of Inequality, Studies in the Social and Cultural Foundations of Language*. Cambridge: Cambridge University Press.

Bassetti, B. (2012). 'Bilingualism and writing systems', in T. K. Bhatia and W. C. Ritchie (eds.) *The Handbook of Bilingualism and Multilingualism*. Hoboken, NJ: John Wiley & Sons, pp. 649–670.

Beeby Lonsdale, A. (1998). 'Direction of translation (directionality)', *Routledge Encyclopedia of Translation Studies*. London and New York: Routledge.

Bell, R. T. (1991). *Translation and Translating*. London and New York: Longman.

Bellos, D. (2016). *Is That a Fish in Your Ear?: The Amazing Adventure of Translation*. London: Penguin.

Bloomfield, L. (1933). *Language*. New York: Holt.

Boase-Beier, J. (2006). *Stylistic Approaches to Translation*. London: Routledge.

Bonfiglio, T. P. (2010). *Mother Tongues and Nations: The Invention of the Native Speaker*. Berlin: Mouton de Gruyter.

Bonfiglio, T. P. (2013). 'The Invention of the native speaker', *Critical Multilingualism Studies: An Interdisciplinary Journal*, 1(2), pp. 29–58.

Bourdieu, P. (1977). *Outline of a Theory of Practice, Outline of a Theory of Practice*. Translated by Richard Nice. Cambridge: Cambridge University Press.

Bruni, L. (1992). 'Extracts from De interpretatione recta (the right way to translate) published in 1420', in Lefevere, A. (ed.), *Translation/History/Culture: A Sourcebook*. London New York: Routledge. pp. 33–35.

Buchweitz, A., and Alves, F. (2006). 'Cognitive adaptation in translation: An interface between language direction, time, and recursiveness in target text production', *Letras de Hoje*, 41(2 SE-Artigos), pp. 81–90.

Burke, P. (2004). '"Speak, that I may see thee": the discovery of language in early modern Europe', in Burke, P. (ed.), *Languages and Communities in Early Modern Europe*. Cambridge: Cambridge University Press (The Wiles Lectures), pp. 15–42.

Burke, P. (2007). 'Translations into Latin in early modern Europe', in Burke, P. and Hsia, R. P.-C. (eds.), *Cultural Translation in Early Modern Europe*. Cambridge: Cambridge University Press, pp. 65–80.

Butler, J. (1990). *Gender Trouble: Feminism and the Subversion of Identity*. New York: Routledge.

Butler, J. (2011). *Bodies that Matter: On the Discursive Limits of Sex*. New York: Taylor & Francis.

Butterfield, A. (2009). *The Familiar Enemy: Chaucer, Language and Nation in the Hundred Years' War*. Oxford: Oxford University Press.

Bybee, J. L. and Hopper, P. J. (2001). 'Introduction to frequency and the emergence of linguistic structure', in Bybee, J. L. and Hopper, P. J. (eds.), *Frequency and the Emergence of Linguistic Structure*. Amsterdam: John Benjamins, pp. 1–26.

Bynum, C. (1986). *Holy Feast and Holy Fast: The Religious Significance of Food to Medieval Women*. Berkeley: University of California Press.

Cameron, D. (2007). 'Language endangerment and verbal hygiene: History, morality and politics', in Duchêne, A. and Heller, M. (eds.), *Discourses of Endangerment: Ideology and Interest in the Defence of Languages*. New York: Bloomsbury, pp. 268–85.

Campbell, S. (1998). *Translation into the Second Language*. London and New York: Longman.

Canagarajah, S. and Liyanage, I. (2012). 'Lessons from pre-colonial multilingualism', in Martin-Jones, M., Blackledge, A., and Creese, A. (eds.), *The Routledge Handbook of Multilingualism*. London: Routledge, pp. 49–65.

Cao, D. (1996). 'Towards a model of translation proficiency', *Target: International Journal of Translation Studies*, 8(2), pp. 325–340.

Catford, J. C. (1965). *A Linguistic Theory of Translation*. London: Oxford University Press.

Chang, V. C.-Y. and Chen, I.-F. (2023). 'Translation directionality and the Inhibitory Control Model: a machine learning approach to an eye-tracking study', *Frontiers in Psychology*, 14.

Chesterman, A. (1997). *Memes of Translation – The Spread of Ideas in Translation Theory*. Amsterdam, Philadelphia: John Benjamins.

Chesterman, A. (2004). 'Beyond the Particular', in Mauranen, A. (ed.), *Translation Universals: Do They Exist?* Amsterdam and Philadelphia: John Benjamins, pp. 33–50.

Chesterman, A. (2007). 'Bridge concepts in translation sociology', in Wolf, M. and Fukari, A. (eds.), *Constructing a Sociology of Translation*. Amsterdam and Philadelphia: John Benjamins, pp. 171–183.

Chesterman, A. (2009). 'The name and nature of translator studies', *Hermes: Journal of Language and Communication Studies*, 22(42), pp. 13–22.

Chomsky, N. (1965). *Aspects of the Theory of Syntax*. Cambridge, MA: MIT Press.

Chow, R. (2014). *Not Like a Native Speaker: On Languaging as a Postcolonial Experience*. New York: Columbia University Press.

Cogo, A. (2012). 'English as a lingua franca: Concepts, use, and implications', *ELT Journal*, 66(1), pp. 97–105.

Collischonn, L. (2023). *With Apologies to My Mother Tongue: L2 Translation as an Exophonic Practice*. Doctoral Thesis, University of Warwick.

Cook, V. J. (1992). 'Evidence for multicompetence', *Language Learning*, 42(4), pp. 557–591.

Cronin, M. (2006). *Translation and Identity*. Abingdon and New York: Routledge.

Cruz Trainor, M. M. de la (2004). 'Traducción inversa: una realidad', *TRANS. Revista de Traductología*, 8, pp. 53–60.

Cummins, J. (1984). 'Wanted: A theoretical framework for relating language proficiency to academic achievement among bilingual students', in Rivera, C. (ed.), *Language Proficiency and Academic Achievement*. Clevedon: Multilingual Matters. pp. 2–19.

Cummins, J. (2000). 'Putting language proficiency in its place: responding to critiques of the conversational/academic language distinction', in Cenoz, J. and Jessner, U. (eds.), *English in Europe: The Acquisition of a Third Language*. Clevedon: Multilingual Matters, pp. 54–83.

da Silva, I. A. L., Alves, F., Schmaltz, M., et al. (2017). 'Translation, post-editing and directionality: A study of effort in the Chinese-Portuguese language pair', in Jakobsen, A. and Mesa-Lao, B. (eds.), *Translation in Transition: Between Cognition, Computing and Technology*. Amsterdam: John Benjamins, pp. 107–134.

Davidson, M. C. (2009). *Medievalism, Multilingualism, and Chaucer*. New York: Palgrave Macmillan US (The New Middle Ages).

Davies, A. (2003). *The Native Speaker: Myth and Reality*. Bristol: Multilingual Matters.

Dawkins, R. (1976). *The Selfish Gene*. Oxford: Oxford University Press.

Di Giovanni, E. and Chelati Dirar, U. (2015). 'Reviewing directionality in writing and translation: Notes for a history of translation in the Horn of Africa', *Translation Studies*, 8(2), pp. 175–190.

Diebold, A. R. (1964). 'Incipient bilingualism', *Language*, 37, pp. 97–112.

Dorostkar, N. (2014). *(Mehr-)Sprachigkeit und Lingualismus: Die diskursive Konstruktion von Sprache im Kontext nationaler und supranationaler Sprachenpolitik am Beispiel Österreichs*. Göttingen: V & R unipress.

Dryden, J. (1992). 'Extracts from his preface to his translation of Ovid's Epistles published in 1680', in Lefevere, A. (ed.), *Translation/History/Culture: A Sourcebook*. London: Routledge, pp. 102–104.

Duff, A. (1989). *Translation*. Oxford: Oxford University Press.

Dziurosz, M. (2017). 'On L2 ("non-native") Translation', *The Linguist*, 1(56), pp. 26–27.

Erasmus, D. (1992). 'Extracts from the "Letter to William Warham," dated 1506', in Lefevere, A. (ed.), *Translation/History/Culture: A Sourcebook*. London: Routledge, pp. 25–31.

References

Espósito, A. P. (1995). 'Bilingualism, philology and the cultural nation: The medieval monolingual imaginary', *Catalan Review*, IX(2), pp. 125–139.

Even-Zohar, I. (1990). 'The position of translated literature within the literary polysystem', *Polysystem Studies – Poetics Today*, 11(1), pp. 45–51.

Ferreira, A. (2014). 'Analyzing recursiveness patterns and retrospective protocols of professional translators in L1 and L2 translation tasks', *Translation and Interpreting Studies*, 9(1), pp. 109–127.

Ferreira, A. and Schwieter, J. W. (2017). 'Directionality in translation', in Schwieter, J. W. and Wei, L. (eds.), *The Handbook of Translation and Cognition*, Hoboken, NJ: Wiley-Blackwell, pp. 90–105.

Ferreira, A. A. (2013). *Direcionalidade em tradução: o papel da subcompetência bilíngue em tarefas de tradução L1 e L2*. Doctoral Thesis. Brazil: Universidade Federal de Minas Gerais, MG.

Fishman, J. A. (1971). 'An interdisciplinary social science approach to language in society', in Fishman, J. A. (ed.), *Advances in the Sociology of Language, Volume 1*. The Hague: Mouton. pp. 217–404.

Fornet, A. (1997). 'Sonar en cubano, escribir en ingles: una reflexión sobre la triada lengua-nación-literatura', *Temas*, 10, pp. 4–12.

Fonseca, N. B. de L. (2014). 'Investigando processos de solução de problemas e tomada de decisão no desempenho de tradutores profissionais durante tarefas de tradução direta e inversa', *Letras de Hoje*, 49(1), pp. 106–116.

Forster, L. (1970). *The Poet's Tongues: Multilingualism in Literature*. London: Cambridge University Press.

Gal, S. (1993). 'Diversity and contestation in linguistic ideologies: German speakers in hungary', *Language in Society*, 22(3), pp. 337–359.

Galbraith, V. H. (1941). 'Nationality and language in medieval England', *Transactions of the Royal Historical Society*, 23, pp. 113–128.

Gilmour, R. (2020). *Bad English: Literature, Multilingualism, and the Politics of Language in Contemporary Britain*. Manchester: Manchester University Press.

Goethe, J. W. (1992). 'Extract from Dichtung und Wahrheit ("Poetry and Truth") written between 1811 and 1814', in Lefevere, A. (ed.), *Translation/History/Culture: A Sourcebook*. London: Routledge.

Gramling, D. (2018). *The Invention of Monolingualism*. London: Bloomsbury Academic.

Gramling, D. (2021). *The Invention of Multilingualism, Key Topics in Applied Linguistics*. Cambridge: Cambridge University Press.

Grosjean, F. (1985). 'The bilingual as a competent but specific speaker-hearer', *Journal of Multilingual and Multicultural Development*, 6(6), pp. 467–477.

Grosjean, F. (1994). 'Individual bilingualism', in Asher, R. E. and Simpson, J. M. (eds.), *The Encyclopedia of Language and Linguistics (Volume 3)*. Oxford: Pergamon. pp. 163–187.

Grosman, M., Kadric, M., Kovaĉiĉ, I., and Snell-Hornby, M. (eds.) (2000). *Translation into Non-mother Tongues in Professional Practice and Training*, Tübingen: Stauffenburg.

Gutt, E.-A. (1990). 'A theoretical account of translation – Without a translation theory', *Target: International Journal of Translation Studies*, 2(2), pp. 135–164.

Hadley, J. and Akashi, M. (2015). 'Translation and celebrity: The translation strategies of Haruki Murakami and their implications for the visibility paradigm', *Perspectives: Studies in Translatology*, 23(3), pp. 458–474.

Hagemann, S. (2019). 'Directionality in translation and revision teaching: a case study of an A–B teacher working with B–A students', *The Interpreter and Translator Trainer*, 13(1), pp. 86–101.

Hamilton, J., Lopes, M., McNamara, T., and Sheridan, E. (1993). 'Rating scales and native speaker performance on a communicatively oriented EAP test', *Language Testing*, 10(3), pp. 337–353.

Hamers, J. F. and Blanc, M. H. A. (2000). *Binguality and Bilingualism*. Cambridge: Cambridge University Press.

Hansegård, N. E. (1975). *Tvåspråkighet eller halvspråkighet?, Series 253*. Stockholm: Aldus.

Harries, P. (1987). 'The roots of ethnicity: Discourse and the politics of language construction in South-East Africa', *African Affairs*, 87, pp. 25–52.

Haugen, E. (1966). 'Language conflict and language planning', *The American Behavioral Scientist*, 10(8), pp. 13–18.

Haugen, E. (1972). *The Ecology of Language*. Stanford: Stanford University Press.

Heilbron, J. (1999). 'Towards a sociology of translation', *European Journal of Social Theory*, 2(4), pp. 429–444.

Herder, J. G. (1992). 'Extracts from the Fragmente (Fragments) published in 1766 and 1767', in Lefevere, A. (ed.), *Translation/History/Culture: A Sourcebook*. London: Routledge, pp. 20–26.

Hermans, T. (1999). *Translation in Systems: Descriptive and Systemic Approaches Explained*. Manchester: St Jerome.

Hermans, T. (2007). 'Translation, irritation and resonance', in Wolf, M. and Fukari, A. (eds.), *Constructing a Sociology of Translation*. Amsterdam and Philadelphia: John Benjamins, pp. 57–75.

Hernández-Chávez, E., Burt, M. and Dulay, H. (1978) 'Language dominance and proficiency testing: Some general considerations', *NABE Journal*, 3(1), pp. 41–54.

Heryanto, A. (1990). 'The Making of Language: Developmentalism in Indonesia', *Prisma; The Indonesian Indicator*, 50, pp. 40–53.

Heryanto, A. (1995). *Language of Development and Development of Language: The Case of Indonesia*. Canberra: Department of Linguistics, Australia National University.

Holliday, A. (2006). 'Native-speakerism', *ELT Journal*, 60(4), pp. 385–387.

Holmes, J. S. (1988). 'The name and nature of translation studies', in Holmes, J. S. (ed.), *Translated! Papers on Literary Translation and Translation Studies*. Amsterdam: Rodopi, pp. 67–80.

Hopper, P. (1998). 'Emergent grammar', in Tomasello, M. (ed.), *The New Psychology of Language*. Mahwah, NJ: Lawrence Erlbaum, pp. 155–175.

Houghton, S. A. and Hashimoto, K. (eds.) (2018). *Towards Post-Native-Speakerism Dynamics and Shifts*. Singapore: Springer.

Hugo, V. (1992). 'Introduction to the translation of Shakespeare', in A. Lefevere (ed.), *Translation/History/Culture: A Sourcebook*. London: Routledge.

Hülmbauer, C., Böhringer, H., and Seidlhofer, B. (2008). 'Introducing English as a lingua franca (ELF): Precursor and partner in intercultural communication', *Synergies Europe*, 3, pp. 25–36.

Hulstijn, J. H. (2015). *Language Proficiency in Native and Non-native Speakers Theory and Research*. Amsterdam: John Benjamins Publishers.

Hur, A. (2018). 'How to write Queer Korean Lit: A manual', *Litro Magazine*, May, www.litromagazine.com/every-saturday-litro-magazine-publishes-essays-that-reach-far-beneath-the-surface/write-queer-korean-lit-manual/. Accessed on 11 January 2022.

Hymes, D.H. (1972). 'On Communicative Competence', in: J. B. Pride and J. Holmes (eds.), *Sociolinguistics. Selected Readings*. Harmondsworth: Penguin, pp. 269–293.

Jamoussi, R. (2015). 'Exporting cultural goods through the medium of translation in the Arab world: The (not so) strange case of L2 translation', *The Translator*, 21(2), pp. 173–188.

Jefferson, J. A., Putter, A., and Hopkins, A. (eds.) (2013). *Multilingualism in Medieval Britain (c. 1066–1520) Sources and Analysis*. Turnhout: Brepols n.v.

Jia, J., Cheng, Z. W. H., and Wang, X. (2023). 'Translation directionality and translator anxiety: Evidence from eye movements in L1-L2 translation', *Frontiers in Psychology*, 14, pp. 51–62.

Johnson, J., and Rosano, T. (1993). Relation of cognitive style to metaphor interpretation and second language proficiency. *Applied Psycholinguistics*, 14, pp. 159–175.

Jones, E. (2022). *Literature in Motion: Translating Multilingualism across the Americas*. New York: Columbia University Press.

Kachru, B. (1992). *The Other Tongue: English across Cultures*. Chicago: University of Illinois Press.

Kaindl, K. (2021). '(Literary) Translator Studies: Shaping the field', in Kaindl, K., Kolb, W., and Schlager, D. (eds.), *Literary Translator Studies*, Amsterdam and Philadelphia: John Benjamins, pp. 1–38.

Karlander, D. and Salö, L. (2023). 'The origin of semilingualism: Nils-Erik Hansegård and the cult of the mother tongue', *Journal of Sociolinguistics*, 27(5), pp. 506–525.

Kelly, D., Nobs, M., Sánchez, D., and Way, C. (eds.) (2003). *La direccionalidad en Traducción e Interpretacion: Perspectivas teóricas, profesionales y didácticas, 2002 Forum on Directionality in Translating and Interpreting in Granada*. Granada: Editorial Atrio.

Kiraly, D. C. (1995). *Pathways to Translation: Pedagogy and Process*. Kent: Kent State University Press.

Kramsch, C. (2003). 'The privilege of the nonnative speaker', *PMLA*, 112, pp. 359–369.

Kroskrity, P. V. (2000). 'Regimenting languages: Language ideological perspectives', in Kroskrity, P. V. (ed.), *Regimes of Language: Ideologies, Politics and Identities*. Santa Fe, NM: School of American Research Press, pp. 1–34.

Kubota, R., and Lin, A. (2009). 'Race, culture, and identities in second language education', in Kubota, R. and Lin, A. (eds.), *Race, Culture and Identities in Second Language Education: Exploring Critically Engaged Practice*. New York: Routledge, pp. 1–23.

Kuzar, R. (2001). *Hebrew and Zionism: A Discourse Analytic Cultural Study*. Berlin and New York: De Gruyter Mouton.

Lamb, S. (1992). 'The sources of linguistic patterning', *LACUS*, XIX, pp. 23–44.

Lennon, B. (2015). 'Challenges to monolingual national literatures', in Kramsch, C. J. and Jessner-Schmid, U. (eds.), *The Multilingual Challenge: Cross-Disciplinary Perspectives*. Berlin: De Gruyter Mouton, pp. 143–160.

Li, W. (2018). 'Translanguaging as a practical theory of language', *Applied Linguistics*, 39(1), pp. 9–30.

Li, W., Milroy, L., and Ching, P. S. (1992). 'A two-step sociolinguistic analysis of codeswitching and language choice: The example of a bilingual Chinese community in Britain', *International Journal of Applied Linguistics*, 2(1), pp. 63–86.

Lindqvist, Y. (2006). 'Consecration mechanisms: The reconstruction of the Swedish Field of High Prestige Literary Translation during the 1980s and 1990s', in Wolf, M. (ed.), *Übersetzen – Translating – Traduire: Towards a 'Social Turn'*. Vienna: LIT Verlag, pp. 65–75.

Litwiller, F. (2020). 'Normative drag culture and the making of precarity', *Leisure Studies*, 39(4), pp. 600–612.

Love, N. L. (2009). 'Science, language, and linguistic culture', *Language & Communication*, 29, pp. 26–46.

Makoni, S. and Pennycook, A. (2006). *Disinventing and Reconstituting Languages*. Clevedon: Multilingual Matters.

Malkiel, B. (2004). 'Directionality and translational difficulty', *Perspectives*, 12(3), pp. 208–219.

Mannheim, B. (1991). *The Language of the Inkha since the European Invasion*. Austin, TX: University of Texas Press.

Marmaridou, A. S. S. (1996). 'Directionality in translation: Processes and practices', *Target: International Journal of Translation Studies*, 8(1), pp. 49–73.

Marsh, G. P. (1859). *Inaugural Addresses of Theodore W. Dwight, Professor of Law, and of George P. Marsh, Professor of English Literature*. New York: Wyn- koop, Hallenbeck & Thomas Printers.

Matter-Seibel, S. (2006). 'Margaret Fullers Übersetzungen deutscher Werke: Soziale Entstehungsbedingungen und genderspezifische Aspekte', in Wolf, M. (ed.), *Übersetzen – Translating – Traduiere: Towards a 'Social Turn'?* Vienna: LIT Verlag, pp. 23–34.

McAlester, G. (1992). 'Teaching translation into a foreign language: Status, scope and aims', in Dollerup, C. and Loddegaard, A. (eds.), *Teaching Translation and Inter-preting: Training, Talent and Experience*. Amsterdam; Philadelphia, PA: John Benjamins, pp. 291–297.

McAlester, G. (2005). 'The evaluation of translation into a foreign language', in Schäffner, C. and Adab, B. (eds.), *Developing Translation Competence*. Amsterdam; Philadelphia, PA: John Benjamins, pp. 229–241.

Mignolo, W. D. (1996). 'Linguistic maps, literary geographies, and cultural landscapes: Languages, languaging, and (trans)nationalism', *Modern Language Quarterly*, 57(2), pp. 181–196.

Mignolo, W. D. (2009). 'Epistemic disobedience, independent thought and decolonial freedom," *Theory, Culture & Society*, 26(7–8), pp. 159–181.

Mignolo, W. D. (2012). *Local Histories/Global Designs*. Princeton: Princeton University Press.

Modiano, M. (2001). 'Ideology and the ELT practitioner', *International Journal of Applied Linguistics*, 11(2), pp. 159–173.

Modiano, M. (2005). 'Cultural studies, foreign language teaching and learning practices, and the NNS practitioner', in Braine, G. (ed.), *Non-native Language Teachers*. New York: Springer, pp. 25–43.

Moore, R. (2013). 'Everything else is drag: Linguistic drag and gender parody on rupaul's drag race', *Journal of Research in Gender Studies*, 3(2), pp. 15–26.

Nelson, L. (1999). 'Bodies (and Spaces) do Matter: The limits of performativity', *Gender, Place & Culture*, 6(4), pp. 331–353.

Neubert, A. and Shreve, G. M. (1992). *Translation as Text*. Kent, OH, and London: The Kent State University Press.

Newmark, P. (1988). *Textbook of Translation*. Hempstead : Prentice Hall.

Newmark, P. (2001). "A translator's approach to literary language" *Across Languages and Cultures*, 2, pp. 5–14.

Niranjana, T. (1992). *Siting Translation: History, Poststructuralism, and the Colonial Context*. Berkeley, CA: University of California Press.

Noorani, Y. (2013). 'Hard and soft multilingualism', *Critical Multilingualism Studies*, 1(2), pp. 7–28.

Nord, C. (2011). 'Making the source text grow: a plea against the idea of loss in translation', in Buffagni, C., Garzelli, B., and Zanotti, S. (ed.), *The Translator as Author: Perspectives on Literary Translation : Proceedings of the International Conference, Universita Per Stranieri of Siena, 28–29 May 2009*. Berlin: LIT Verlag, pp. 21–30.

Oller, J. W. and Perkins, K. (1980). *Research in Language Testing*. Rowley, MA: Newbury House.

Ortega, L. (2013). 'SLA for the twenty first century: Disciplinary progress, trans-disciplinary relevance, and the bi/multilingual turn', *Language Learning*, 63(s1), pp. 1–24.

Parks, T. (2010). 'The Dull New Global Novel', *The New York Review*, February. Link: www.nybooks.com/online/2010/02/09/the-dull-new-global-novel/. Accessed on 20th May 2022.

Pavlović, N. (2007). *Directionality in Collaborative Translation Processes: A Study of Novice Translators*. (PhD Thesis). Tarragona: Universitat Rovira i Virgili

Pearson, B. Z. (2010). 'We can no longer afford a monolingual norm', *Applied Psycholinguistics*, 31(2), pp. 339–343.

Pennycook, A. (2004). 'Performativity and language studies', *Critical Inquiry in Language Studies*, 1(1), pp. 1–19.

Pennycook, A. and Makoni, S. (2012). 'Disinventing multilingualism: From monological multilingualism to multilingua Francas', in Martin-Jones, M., Blackledge, A., and Creese, A. (eds.), *The Routledge Handbook of Multilingualism*. London: Routledge, pp. 439–453.

Petrova, E. (2020). 'Neither Here And There: The Misery And Splendor Of (Reverse) Translation*', *Reading in Translation*, July, p. online. Accessed on 3 August 2020: https://readingintranslation.com/2020/07/28/neither-here-and-there-the-misery-and-splendor-of-reverse-translation/.

Phipps, A. (2013). 'Unmoored: language pain, porosity, and poisonwood', *Critical Multilingualism Studies*, 1(2), pp. 96–118.

Pietryga, M. (2022). "Perception of directionality in translation Among students," *Acta Neophilologica*, 1(XXIV), pp. 87–110.

Pokorn, N. (2005). *Challenging the Traditional Axioms Translation into a Non-mother Tongue*. Amsterdam; Philadelphia, PA: John Benjamins.

Pratt, M. L. (1987). 'Linguistic Utopias', in Fabb, N. and Al, E. (eds.), *The Linguistics of Writing*. Manchester: Manchester University Press, pp. 48–66.

Prunč, E. (2003). 'Óptimo, subóptimo, fatal: refelexiones sobre la democracia etnolingüística en la cultura europea de traducción', in D. Kelly, A. Martin, M.-L. Nobs et al. (eds.), *La direcconalidad en traducción e interpretación: perspectivas teóreticas, profesionales y didácticas*. Granada: Editorial Atrio, pp. 67–89.

Prunč, E. (2007). 'Priests, princes and pariahs: Constructing the professional field of translation', in Wolf, M. and Fukari, A. (eds.), *Constructing a Sociology of Translation*. Amsterdam and Philadelphia: John Benjamins, pp. 39–56.

Pym, A. (1996). 'Ideologies of the expert in discourses on translator training', In Snell-Hornby, M. and Gambier, Y. (ed.), *Problems and Trends in the Teaching of Interpreting and Translation* (= Koinè Anno IV). Misano: Istituto San Pellegrino pp. 139–149.

Pym, A. (1998). *Method in Translation History*. Manchester: St. Jerome

Pym, A. (2003). Redefining Translation Competence in an Electronic Age. *Defence of a Minimalist Approach Meta*, 48(4), pp. 481–497.

UNESCO. *Records of the General Conference, Nineteenth Session, Nairobi, 26 October to 30 November 1976, v. 1: Resolutions* (no date). Nairobi, Kenya: UNESCO.

Rivers, D. J. (2018). 'The idea of the native speaker', in Houghton, S. A., Rivers, D. J., and Hashimoto, K. (eds.), *Beyond Native-Speakerism: Current Explorations and Future Visions*. New York: Routledge, pp. 15–35.

Rogers, M. (2015). *Specialised Translation: Shedding the 'Non-Literary' Tag*. Palgrave Studies in Translating and Interpreting. Basingstoke: Palgrave Macmillan

Rogers, M. (2018). 'From binaries to borders: literary and non-literary translation', In Dam, H., Vrønning, M., Brøgger, N., and Zethsen, N. (eds.), *Moving Boundaries in Translation Studies*. London: Routledge. pp. 151–167.

Rosa, J. and Flores, N. (2017). 'Unsettling race and language: Toward a raciolinguistic perspective', *Language in Society*, 46(5), pp. 621–647.

Samuelsson-brown, G. (1995). *A Practical Guide for Translators*. Clevedon: Multilingual Matters.

Schleiermacher, F. (1963). 'Über die verschiedenen Methoden des Übersezens (1813)', in Störig, H. (ed.), *Das Problem des Übersetzens*. Stuttgart: Henry Goverts, pp. 38–70.

Schögler, R. (2017). 'Sociology of translation', in Odell Korgen, K. (ed.), *The Cambridge Handbook of Sociology, Volume 2*. Cambridge: Cambridge University Press, pp. 399–407.

Schweiger, H. (2006). 'Habituelle Divergenzen: Siegfried Trebitsch als Übersetzer und Vermittler George Bernard Shaws [Habitual divergencies: Siegried Trebitsch as translator and George Bernard Shaw intermediary]', in Wolf, M. (ed.), *Übersetzen - translating - traduire: towards a 'social turn'?* (Repräsentation-Transformation: Translating across Cultures and Societies 1). Münster: LIT Verlag, pp. 45–54.

Sela-Sheffy, R. (2016). 'Elite and non-elite translator manpower: The non-professionalised culture in the translation field in Israel', *The Journal of Specialised Translation*, 25, pp. 54–73.

Shin, H. (신혜정) (2022). 'Comparing L1 and L2 translation styles: An analysis of multiple parallel corpora comprised of multiple target texts of the same source texts', *Journal of International Culture*, 15(2), pp. 67–88.

Sieg, K. (2002). *Ethnic Drag: Performing Race, Nation, Sexuality in West Germany*. Ann Harbor: University of Michigan Press.

Simeoni, D. (1998). 'The Pivotal Status of the Translator's Habitus'. *Target*, 10(1), pp. 1–39.

Skutnabb-Kangas, T. (1981). *Bilingualism or Not: The Education of Minorities*. Clevedon: Multilingual Matters.

Skutnabb-Kangas, T. and Toukomaa, P. (1976). *Teaching Migrant Children Mother Tongue and Learning the Language of the Host Country in the Context of the Socio-Cultural Situation of the Migrant Family*. Tampere, Finland: Tukimuksia Research Reports.

Snell-Hornby, M. (1992). 'The professional translator of tomorrow: Language specialist or all-round expert?', in Dollerup, C. and Loddegaard, A. (eds.), *Teaching Translation and Interpreting: Training, Talent and Experience*. Amsterdam and Philadelphia: John Benjamins, pp. 9–22.

Spitzer, L. ([1942]1968). *Essays in Historical Semantics*. New York: Russell & Russell.

Spivak, G. C. (1988). 'Can the subaltern speak?', in Nelson, C. and Grossberg, L. (eds.), *Marxism and the Interpretation of Culture*. Basingstoke: Macmillan, pp. 271–313.

Stasimioti, M., Sosoni, V., and Chatzitheodorou, K. (2021). 'Investigating post-editing effort', *Cognitive Linguistic Studies*, 8(2), pp. 378–403.

Stern, H. H. (1992). *Issues and Options in Language Teaching*. Oxford: Oxford University Press.

Stewart, D. (2001). 'Poor relations and black sheep in translation studies', *Target*, 12(2), pp. 205–228.

Stoklosinski, E. (2014). *Another View Tracing the Foreign in Literary Translation*. Champaign IL: Dalkey Archive Press.

Suga, K. (2007). 'Translation, exophony, omniphony', in Slaymaker, D. (ed.), *Yoko Tawada: Voices from Everywhere*. Lanham, MD: Lexington Books. pp. 21–34

Swain, M. (2006). 'Languaging, agency and collaboration in advanced second language learning', in Byrnes, H. (ed.), *Advanced Language Learning: The Contributions of Halliday and Vygotsky*. London: Continuum, pp. 95–108.

Tawada, Y. (2003). *Ekusofonii: bogo no soto e deru tabi (エクソフォニー——母語の外へ出る旅)*. Tokyo: Iwanami.

Toury, G. (1995). *Descriptive Translation Studies and Beyond*. Amsterdam, Philadelphia, PA: John Benjamins.

Treffers-Daller, J. (2018). 'The measurement of Bilingual abilities', in De Houwer, A. and Ortega, L. (eds.), *The Cambridge Handbook of Bilingualism*. Cambridge: Cambridge University Press (Cambridge Handbooks in Language and Linguistics), pp. 289–306.

Valdes, G. and Figueroa, R. A. (1994). *Bilingualism and Testing: A Special Case of Bias*. Norwood, NJ: Ablex.

Venuti, L. (1998). *The Scandals of Translation: Towards an Ethics of Difference*. London: Routledge.

Vermeer, H. J. (1978). 'Ein Rahmen für eine allgemeine Translationstheorie', *Lebende Sprachen*, 23(3), pp. 99–102.

Wacquant, L. (2018). 'A Concise Genealogy and Anatomy of Habitus', in Medvetz, T. and Sallaz, J. J. (eds.), *The Oxford Handbook of Pierre Bourdieu*. Oxford: Oxford University Press, pp. 529–536.

Wang, B. (2009). 'The issue of direction of translation in China: A historical overview', *Translation Journal*, 13(3). www.translationjournal.net/journal/49direction.htm .

Wang, B. (2011). 'Translation practices and the issue of directionality in China', *Meta*, 56(4), pp. 896–914.

Wang, L. (Evelyn) and Fang, F. (Gabriel) (2020). 'Native-speakerism policy in English language teaching revisited: Chinese university teachers' and students' attitudes towards native and non-native English-speaking teachers', *Cogent Education*, 7(1), p. 1778374.

Whyatt, B. (2019). 'In search of directionality effects in the translation process and in the end product', *Translation, Cognition & Behavior*, 2(1), pp. 79–100.

Wolf, M. (1999). 'Zum "sozialen Sinn" in der Translation: Translationssoziologische Implikationen von Pierre Bourdieus Kultursoziologie', *Arcadia*, 34(2), pp. 262–275.

Wolf, M. (2002). 'Culture as translation – and beyond: Ethnographic models of representation in translation studies', in Hermans, T. (ed.), *Crosscultural Transgressions. Research Models in Translation Studies II: Historical and Ideological Issues*. Manchester: St Jerome, pp. 180–192.

Wolf, M. (2003). 'Translating – a social event: Towards a sociological approach of translation', in Bonito Couto Pereira, H. and Guarnieri Atik, M. L. (eds.), *Língua, Literatura e Cultura em Diálogo*. São Paulo: Editora Mackenzie, pp. 47–67.

Wolf, M. (2007). 'The emergence of a sociology of translation', in Wolf, M. and Fukari, A. (eds.), *Constructing a Sociology of Translation*. Amsterdam; Philadelphia, PA: John Benjamins, pp. 1–36.

Woolard, K. A. (2002). 'Bernardo de Aldrete and the Morisco Problem: A study in early modern Spanish language ideology', *Comparative Studies in Society and History*, 44(3), pp. 446–480.

Wright, C. (2008). 'Writing in the "Grey Zone": Exophonic Literature in Contemporary Germany', *gfl- journal*, 3, pp. 25–41.

Wright, C. (2010). 'Exophony and literary translation: What it means for the translator when a writer adopts a new language', *Target*, 22(1), pp. 22–39.

Wright, C. (2013). *Yoko Tawada's Portrait of a Tongue*. Ottawa: University of Ottawa Press.

Wright, C. (2016). *Literary Translation*. London and New York: Routledge.

Yildiz, Y. (2012). *Beyond the Mother Tongue – The Postmonolingual Condition*. New York: Fordham University Press.

Zahedi, S. (2013). 'L2 translation at the periphery: A meta-analysis of current views on translation directionality', *TranscUlturAl*, 5(1–2), pp. 43–60.

Zaliwska-Okrutna, U. (2008) 'Translator-centred view on translation', in Thielen, M. and Lewandowska-Tomaszczyk, B. (eds.), *Translation and Meaning, Part 8 – Proceedings of the Łódź Session of the 4th International Maastricht – Łódź Duo Colloquium on 'Translation and Meaning', Held in Łódź, Poland, 23 – 25 September 2005*. Maastricht: UPM, Universitaire Pers Maastricht, pp. 107–114.

Cambridge Elements

Translation and Interpreting

The series is edited by Kirsten Malmkjær with Sabine Braun as associate editor for Elements focusing on Interpreting.

Kirsten Malmkjær
University of Leicester

Kirsten Malmkjær is Professor Emeritus of Translation Studies at the University of Leicester. She has taught Translation Studies at the universities of Birmingham, Cambridge, Middlesex and Leicester and has written extensively on aspects of both the theory and practice of the discipline. *Translation and Creativity* (London: Routledge) was published in 2020 and *The Cambridge Handbook of Translation*, which she edited, was published in 2022. She is preparing a volume entitled *Introducing Translation* for the Cambridge Introductions to Language and Linguistics series.

Editorial Board

Adriana Serban, *Université Paul Valéry*
Barbara Ahrens, *Technische Hochschule Köln*
Liu Min-Hua, *Hong Kong Baptist University*
Christine Ji, *The University of Sydney*
Jieun Lee, *Ewha Womans University*
Lorraine Leeson, *The University of Dublin*
Sara Laviosa, *Università Delgi Stuidi di Bari Aldo Moro*
Fabio Alves, *FALE-UFMG*
Moira Inghilleri, *University of Massachusetts Amherst*
Akiko Sakamoto, *University of Portsmouth*
Haidee Kotze, *Utrecht University*

About the Series

Elements in Translation and Interpreting present cutting edge studies on the theory, practice and pedagogy of translation and interpreting. The series also features work on machine learning and AI, and human-machine interaction, exploring how they relate to multilingual societies with varying communication and accessibility needs, as well as text-focused research.

Cambridge Elements

Translation and Interpreting

Elements in the Series

Navigating the Web
Claire Y. Shih

The Graeco-Arabic Translation Movement
El-Hussein AY Aly

Interpreting as Translanguaging
Lili Han, Zhisheng (Edward) Wen and Alan James Runcieman

Creative Classical Translation
Paschalis Nikolaou

Translation as Creative–Critical Practice
Delphine Grass

Translation in Analytic Philosophy
Francesca Ervas

Towards Game Translation User Research
Mikołaj Deckert, Krzysztof W. Hejduk, and Miguel Á. Bernal-Merino

Hypertranslation
Mª Carmen África Vidal Claramonte and Tong King Lee

An Extraordinary Chinese Translation of Holocaust Testimony
Meiyuan Zhao

Researching and Modelling the Translation Process
Muhammad M. M. Abdel Latif

Risk Management in Translation
Anthony Pym

Literary Exophonic Translation
Lúcia Collischonn

A full series listing is available at: www.cambridge.org/EITI

For EU product safety concerns, contact us at Calle de José Abascal, 56–1°,
28003 Madrid, Spain or eugpsr@cambridge.org.

www.ingramcontent.com/pod-product-compliance
Lightning Source LLC
Chambersburg PA
CBHW071759170625
28357CB00021B/755